# THE DILEMMA OF THE MORAL CURRICULUM IN A CHINESE SECONDARY SCHOOL

## Hongping Annie Nie

University Press of America,® Inc.
Lanham · Boulder · New York · Toronto · Plymouth, UK

**Copyright © 2008 by**
**University Press of America®, Inc.**
4501 Forbes Boulevard
Suite 200
Lanham, Maryland 20706
UPA Acquisitions Department (301) 459-3366

Estover Road
Plymouth PL6 7PY
United Kingdom

All rights reserved
Printed in the United States of America
British Library Cataloging in Publication Information Available

Library of Congress Control Number: 2008920153
ISBN-13: 978-0-7618-4024-4 (clothbound : alk. paper)
ISBN-10: 0-7618-4024-9 (clothbound : alk. paper)
ISBN-13: 978-0-7618-4025-1 (paperback : alk. paper)
ISBN-10: 0-7618-4025-7 (paperback : alk. paper)

♾™ The paper used in this publication meets the minimum
requirements of American National Standard for Information
Sciences—Permanence of Paper for Printed Library Materials,
ANSI Z39.48—1984

# CONTENTS

# ACKNOWLEDGMENTS

This book was inconceivable without the generous support from many people. I am especially grateful to my advisor Dr. Donald Douglas who has guided me over the course of several years from the inception of this study to its completion. He is an exceptional mentor and his influence on me extends well beyond my academic career.

I would also like to thank Dr. Douglas Hayward and Dr. Neonora Douglas at Biola University, Dr. Lee-Beng Chua and Dr. Jennifer Chen at Harvard Graduate School of Education, who have kindly read the drafts and given me invaluable suggestions. Dr. Yusong Chen has provided generous support for my statistical analysis. My editors Ms Maria Giannuzzi and Ms Susan Peabody have made this book presentable and easier to read and understand.

My gratitude also goes to my families. My parents and siblings in China have supported me especially during my field study. Frank and Wilma Huyser, who have become my families in America, have always trust my competence when I lack confidence and motivation. Marvin and Evelyn Anderson have given me a home away from home to finish my last draft, where my daughter was born. To my husband Samuel and our children Gabriel and Juliana I owe my greatest debt and gratitude. Their grace and sacrifice has brought forth the birth of this book.

Finally, my gratitude goes to the teachers and students portrait in this study, to whom this book is dedicated. I have been blessed with your trust and friendship. They are not only the subjects but also the greatest facilitators of this study. To some extent, they share the authorship of this book. My desire to protect their anonymity prevents me from naming them individually. However, their voices and faces have been printed into my heart.

# 1

## INTRODUCTION

### Background

The ideological and moral condition and the quality of scientific knowledge of the students produced by our schools at present and in the future twenty years will directly affect the look of China, whether the strategic goals of the socialist reconstruction can be realized and whether the Party's fundamental line can be sustained for one hundred years. It is necessary to understand the importance of school moral education in the new era from a historic and strategic perspective. (The Chinese Communist Party Central Committee [CCPCC] 1994)

Moral education as a means of ideological and moral inculcation has always been an important concern of the Chinese government. During the reform period as China transforms itself from a socialist planned economy to a socialist market economy there is a mix of conflicting ideologies, values and cultures in emerging Chinese society (Z. Li 1997). Moral education has become an increasingly challenging task. In order to adjust moral education to the new situation in the reform era, the Chinese government began to reform moral education beginning in the 1980s.

The Chinese government's persistent emphasis on moral education is evident when one looks at a series of official directives on the reform of moral education issued by the CCPCC and State Council during the past two decades. These include *A Notice Issued by the CCPCC Regarding the Reformation and Strengthening of Moral Education Work in Elementary and Secondary Schools* (CCPCC 1989), *Suggestions of the CCPCC on*

*Further Strengthening and Improving School Moral Education Work* (CCPCC 1994), and *Suggestions of the Executive Office of the CCPCC and the Executive Office of State Council on Further Strengthening and Improving Moral Education Work in Elementary and Secondary Schools under New Situation* (CCPCC and State Council 2001).

As a result of the implementation of a series of policies developed by the State Education Commission [SEC] (which later became the Ministry of Education) beginning in the 1980s, moral education in schools has become more systematic with specific regulations for the students and general guidelines for the practitioner. These include operational regulations for moral education work in elementary and secondary schools (1998a), the guideline for secondary school moral education (1998b), daily behavior standards for elementary school students (1998c), daily behavior standards for secondary school students (1998d), and regulations for secondary school students and elementary school students (1998e).

However, such emphasis and regulations have not necessarily resulted in improvements in moral education outcomes in schools. In fact, many problems addressed in earlier government policy documents remain unsolved and solutions continue to be called for in later documents. For example, there has long been a nation-wide phenomenon of giving academic teaching priority over moral education. In 1994 the CCPCC called for efforts to overcome both the lack of consistency in Chinese schools (*yishouying, yishouruan,* firmness on one hand, laxity on the other) and the schools' neglect of moral education. Recently, the same problem was noted again. It is suggested that moral education as currently taught in elementary and secondary schools is not appropriate in light of the new developments in Chinese society and that one of the major problems contributing to moral education's ineffectiveness is the overemphasis on academic teaching over moral education in some schools (CCPCC and State Council 2001).

Over two decades after Deng Xiaoping initiated economic reform in China, despite the implementation of numerous reform policies and much official rhetoric, the condition of moral education in Chinese schools is not satisfactory. Students complain moral education is boring and meaningless while moral education workers try to change their professions. Parents, sociologists and many others are concerned about the decline of morality and the increasing crime rate among youth. Even Deng (1990) stated that despite China's great economic growth, the biggest failure of the reform program was ideological and political education.

Studies conducted by Chinese researchers as well as by Western researchers suggest that moral education in Chinese schools is rather problematic (Baken 1991, 2000; Chan 1997; Z. Li 1997; Meyer 1990; Price 1992; Shao 1996; Thogerson 1990). As Merry Jean Chan (1997), a Chinese-American researcher observes, moral education in Chinese schools fails to transform the student moral framework into the desired patriotic, collectivist and socialist moral framework.

However, the factors contributing to the failure or problems of moral education in Chinese schools is still a controversial topic among scholars. Some argue the traditional moral education approach, which focuses on socialization of individuals through imitation and group reinforcement (Hu 1998), is no longer suitable in the current historical period. Some blame the conflicting ideologies and the contradiction between the values transmitted at school and the social and economic realities of the larger Chinese society. Still others suggest that the low standards of professional ethics exhibited by the educators teaching moral education are to blame.

Some researchers believe that the problems of moral education are closely related to the dilemmas that exist in contemporary Chinese society. Z. Li (1997) argues that moral education suffers from a moral crisis at the present time. China is an emerging modern society where new and old value systems conflict with each other. Chinese people find themselves caught between conflicting ideologies, values and cultures. There is a confusion of moral standards among Chinese people, and immoral behaviors have become rampant due to the loosening of social control. Therefore, moral ideals preached at schools largely contradict the social reality; the content of moral education lacks consistency and stability; those involved in moral educational practice lack sincerity; and functionalism in moral education is severe.

It is a well-accepted notion among Western observers that China's economic reform has created a paradox in Chinese society (Fewsmith 1999; Goldman and MacFarquhar 1999; Goldman and Nathan 2000; White 1995; Yeh 1988). These observers believe that, as Chinese society becomes increasingly open, individuals, especially among the younger generation, become more independent minded. While the nation's economy is expanding, the legitimacy of the regime and its control over ideological issues are declining. The indoctrination of the desired ideology among youth is no longer effective in post-reform China. It is fair to say the dilemmas of the emerging Chinese society have posed great challenges to moral education in Chinese schools.

This study investigates students' attitudes toward the moral education curriculum as taught at Central High School [pseudonym], a state-run regular secondary school located in the southwest of China. It seeks to determine how the students respond to the moral education curriculum and why. Student's attitudes are examined at two different levels of the moral education curriculum: the intended moral curriculum and the taught moral curriculum. The current study offers a student perspective to the understanding of the phenomenon of Chinese secondary school moral education from a student perspective. Education in China has long followed a top-down pattern under central government control, with a strong teacher-centered orientation. Traditionally, little attention was given to students' active roles in the learning and teaching process and students had very little say in the process of education reform and policymaking. This helps explain why there is so little literature on moral education from a student perspective.

In the past two decades the Chinese government has attempted to shift moral education in a more decentralized and student-centered direction as seen in official government policy documents on moral education issued since 1978. Despite the resurgence of ideological control in various policy documents, Lee (1996) identifies a continuity of policy statements favoring student-centered teaching, which is expressed in such terms as "developmental needs of the students, self-initiative, self-education, independent thinking, rational teaching, and so on" (p. 11). As a result of this shift to student-centered teaching, it has become increasingly important to enhance the understanding of moral education from a student perspective. Therefore, this study explores how the students respond to the moral education curriculum and the ecological factors that shape those responses and attitudes. It is my hope that the current study will yield insights that will help Chinese policymakers and educational practitioners gain a better understanding of current moral education curriculum as seen through students' eyes and adjust their policy and practice so that moral education will truly benefit the development of the students.

This study also intends to expand the ecological theory of human development within the context of moral education in a Chinese secondary school. Moral education in China is a complicated phenomenon involving numerous factors at different ecological system levels. It is impossible to understand students' attitudes toward the moral education curriculum without considering such contributing factors. For example, the change in the government's moral education policy is largely a reflection of the ideological, political and social changes occurring in Chinese society (Lee 1996). It therefore becomes crucial to study the topic of moral education within the social milieu in which it takes place.

The application of ecological theory of human development enables this study to capture the complexity of the phenomenon of moral education in China. Other theories on moral and ideological education can only be applied to one particular aspect of the complex issue of moral education in China. For example, while psychoanalytical theory mainly addresses the psychological process of moral and ideological learning, social learning theory stresses the behavioral aspect of individuals in their moral and ideological learning. However, through the framework of ecological theory, this study is able to present a more holistic view of the issue of moral education in China within its social context, shedding light on numerous environmental factors that impact moral education and shape students' attitudes toward the moral education curriculum in contemporary Chinese secondary schools.

While seeking to understand how the students respond to the moral education curriculum and why, this study provides a rich description of a particular Chinese secondary school. It takes a qualitative approach in describing the practice of moral education within the total function of a state-run regular secondary school in Southwest China. Although there have been several ethnographic studies of Chinese schools, the literature on moral education is still relatively scanty. In fact, to date the current study is one of the few ethnographic studies devoted to the understanding of moral education in regular secondary schools in China.

The current study has great personal significance. I was born in China during the Cultural Revolution. I spent most of my elementary and junior secondary school years engaged in political activities and learning from workers in the factories and peasants in the countryside. When Deng Xiaoping returned to power, I was about to graduate from secondary school. Like many other students of my generation, I have greatly benefited from Deng's reform policies, especially the reestablishment of national college entrance examinations and the shift in educational focus from political orientation to academic performance. I was able to attend a three-year teachers' college, a two-year program in education at an adult higher learning institution, and finally came to the United States to continue my study.

During my years of graduate study in the United States, I have been closely watching the developments in Chinese education. I have observed that China's educational system has undergone major reforms, producing significant changes, such as increased student enrollment in higher education, the development of vocational education, adult education and private education, as well as an increasing interest in educational research.

However, moral education in Chinese secondary schools has shown little improvement and the content and approach to moral education remains unchanged two decades after Deng's reforms. Since the early 1990s, Chinese scholars and educators have debated the conflicting values in contemporary China and the failure of moral education.

As an educator trained in America with personal experience in the Chinese school system, I would like to contribute to the discussion of the issues affecting moral education in contemporary China. Besides the educational research skills I have learned in the West, I offer my unique perspective on Chinese moral education both as an insider and an outsider. I hope that my personal experience in China, not only as an observer but also as a student and later as a teacher/researcher in the Chinese school system, will bring a broader perspective and deeper understanding of moral education in China in terms of Chinese educational philosophy and practice. At the same time, I have benefited from cross-cultural concepts that have allowed me to better understand and explain moral education issues. In addition, my study of moral education from a Western perspective has helped me to overcome the blind spots and limitations that frequently affect an insider.

## Terminology

Moral education, also called *deyu jiaoyu* in Chinese, refers to a component of public education that teaches or delivers, purposely and in a planned way, certain social ideology and morality, and further makes these social values part of the individual's personal and moral character (Jia Wang 1985). *De* means virtue or morality, *yu* means nurturing.

The Chinese *deyu* is often literally translated as moral education in the West. However, moral education in China differs from moral education in the West. The distinction lies in the unique Chinese conception of virtue or morality.

Morality in the Chinese context is described as "the entity of norms and principles of conduct that is regulated by the particular society, reinforced by its propaganda and relied on in the individual's inner motives" (Wang and Li 1985:47). Morality in China is conditioned by the interest of a certain social class and has a strong political and ideological connotation.

Morality in the Chinese context is also considered to be continuously evolving throughout human history; as a result, there are various types of morality, such as feudalist morality, capitalist morality, and socialist morality or communist morality. It is believed that socialist or communist morality, with its core of collectivism and the spirit of serving the people, is the most advanced morality in human history (Wang and Li 1985).

According to Lee (1996), moral education in China is sometimes called ideological education or political education, and moral qualities are sometimes called ideological-moral qualities.

These terms are interchangeably used in the literature, and they are conceptually intertwined with one another. The connotation of the term also suggests that moral education is directive in nature; that is, it has been seen by the central government as a means of transmitting ideological and political values. (p. 5)

As Meyer (1990) states in his writing on Chinese moral education,

> By "moral education," I mean all those aspects of the educational process, which go beyond the purely cognitive, and are included in the idea of character formation. Therefore, "moral education" includes within its scope the development of personal ethics, character building and ideological formation. (p. 5)

Such a definition succinctly captures the major characteristic of Chinese moral education, which distinguishes it from its Western counterpart. It is obvious that moral education (*deyu*) covers a much broader area. As a pedagogic term, moral education is broad enough to include ideological education, political education and moral education (M. Li 1990). To some extent, moral education in China is equivalent to value/character education plus some courses in social studies and history in American schools.

The working definition of moral education in this study is formulated by combining Meyer's definition with the official Chinese definition. It refers to "all those aspects of the educational process, which go beyond the purely cognitive" and which are intended to mold students into qualified socialist successors possessing officially accepted ideology, correct political thoughts and appropriate moral principles within the Chinese school system. *[definition of moral ed.]*

Thus, politics, ideology, and morality have remained the major elements of moral education in China. According to the guideline for moral education in secondary schools (SEC 1998b), the content of the moral education curriculum for both junior secondary schools and senior secondary schools includes the teaching of patriotism, collectivism, socialism, ideals, morality, concepts of labor, socialist democracy and adherence to laws and regulations, sound personality and psychological traits. The teaching of the *[content]* principles of Marxism and social practice is also included in the moral education curriculum for senior secondary schools, although it is not required for junior secondary schools.

Ideology is an important aspect of moral education in China. The term ideology first appeared in English in 1796 as "the science of ideas, in order to distinguish it from the ancient metaphysics" (Reymond 1985:153–154). It has been used both conservatively and critically in modern times. In its conservative use, ideology is defined as merely illusion, abstract and false thought; in its critical use, ideology is the real knowledge of material and relationships. Later Lenin used ideology to refer to the system of ideas appropriate to a certain class, such as proletarian ideology or bourgeois ideology, and therefore, one ideology can be claimed as correct and progressive as against another ideology.

In this study, the term ideology refers to the official guideline that governs the CCP and the People's Republic of China. Two major ideologies have been at work at different times in contemporary China. One is Marxism combined with Maoism, which dominated China for three decades until 1978 when Deng initiated the period of reform.

Marxist ideology is composed of Marxist philosophy (i.e., dialectical materialism and historical materialism), Marxist political economy, and scientific socialism. In Marxist theory, human society develops in a fixed pattern from the primitive, through slavery and feudal and capitalist societies and ultimately to a communist society. In a capitalist society there are only two antagonists, i.e., the bourgeoisie or capitalist class (those who own the means of production) and the proletariat or working class (the exploited labor class). In the struggle of the two classes the proletariat will win in the end and create a new society, the socialist society. According to the Marxist concept of politics, economics is the foundation of a society and politics is the concentrated statement of economics; therefore politics is the struggle through which one strives for more interest on behalf of one's own class (M. Li 1990).

Mao (1971) contextualized Marxist theory in Chinese society. Mao believed that political work is extremely crucial in Chinese socialist construction and that the focus of politics is class struggle. Basically, Mao's ideology is an ideology of political struggle.

The other official ideology is Deng's (1994) theory on socialism with Chinese characteristics. Deng reinterprets Marxism and Mao's (1971) ideology. Deng believes that China is still at the early stage of socialism, and therefore, the CCP should focus its work on economic development instead of on class struggle. Furthermore, Deng advocates a socialist market economy in his reform program. The essence of Deng's socialism with Chinese Characteristics is a hybrid of a market economy and reconstruction of a socialist spiritual civilization. Deng's theory prevailed during the reform period and continues into the present post-reform era. In fact, socialism with Chinese Characteristics was written into the CCP Constitution as a major guideline under Jiang Zemin's leadership.

As mentioned earlier, this study seeks to understand how students respond to the moral education curriculum and why. Selecting a particular school as a self-contained system enabled me to study in-depth the role of moral education at play and made the task of investigation manageable.

Schofield (1990) argues that one of the approaches to increase generalizability as perceived by qualitative researchers is to study "what is," that is, "to study the typical, the common or the ordinary" (p. 209). She suggests that site selection based on typicality is far more likely to increase the potential generalizability of the study than choosing a site on the basis of convenience or easy access. By choosing a typical case, the researcher "maximizes the fit between the research site and what is more broadly in society" (p. 210).

A secondary school in the southwest of China was chosen as the site of the case study. It is given the pseudonym Central High School in order to protect the school and informants. It is a state-run secondary school that enrolls 1,325 students ranging from grade seven to grade twelve, 132 teaching staff and 31 administrative workers. Its 11,234-square-meter campus holds a recently constructed four-floor building, a couple of old buildings and a small playground. The school enrolls students through a city-wide computer-generated database based on the student's examination scores. Since it is not one of the key schools in the city, the school also takes below or about average students among the same age group from nearby neighborhoods. Every year only a few graduates of Central High School pass the competitive national college entrance examination to pursue higher education. The majority of the graduates either go on to other schools or programs geared toward vocational training or enter the job market.

Central High School was chosen as the site of the case study because it appears to exhibit characteristics of many if not most secondary schools in China. First of all, education system reforms have brought about an increase in the number of vocational and private secondary schools. Among the 111,100 secondary schools in 1997, there were 80,100 regular secondary schools, 17,100 vocational secondary schools and 1,702 private secondary schools (Z. Chen 1999). Despite the increase in vocational and private secondary schools, it is obvious that state-run regular secondary schools form the largest segment of Chinese secondary schools. Central High School was selected for this case study because it is a regular secondary school and therefore representative of this segment.

Secondly, Central High School was selected because it is a non-key school. China's educational system is split by the existence of government-designated key schools and non-key schools. In 1978 Deng Xiaoping reestablished key schools that gather the most talented students and teachers and garner a large portion of government funding, in order to achieve the most effective use of limited educational resources. There are several categories of key schools, such as provincial key schools, city key schools and county key schools. In general, key schools have a much higher percentage of graduates entering universities and colleges than non-key schools. However, such elite schools comprise a very small percentage of schools in China's educational system. As a non-key regular secondary school run by the state, Central High School can be considered one of "the typical, the common or the ordinary" (Schofield 1990:209). By investigating students' attitudes towards moral education curriculum at Central High School, this study seeks to provide information that will contribute to an understanding of how Chinese secondary students in general respond to moral education curriculum at their schools.

Thirdly, the level of educational development in Chinese secondary schools varies geographically. On one end of the spectrum are modern schools in the highly developed coastal areas. On the other end of the spectrum are run-down schools in remote areas of China where resources are scarce. Central High School, situated in a moderately developed inland city, fits in the middle of the spectrum. Unlike the two extremes, which represent the most advanced schools and least advanced schools in the area of educational reform, Central High School resembles the majority of Chinese secondary schools of its type in its depth and breadth of educational development.

In addition, Central High School was chosen for this study because I am familiar with the school and its surrounding environment. I lived for 20 years in a neighborhood near Central High School before I came to the United States. Although I attended another secondary school, my sister and my niece as well as some of my friends attended Central High School. My familiarity with the city and the school gave me an in-depth understanding of the phenomenon of moral education in a specific setting.

Finally, I chose Central High School as the site of the study because of the support from the school. In China it can be difficult for a person from overseas to obtain entry into any institutions to conduct research, especially in the field of social studies. Applying for official permission can be a complicated process, involving much paperwork, a long waiting period, and the likelihood of rejection. On the other hand, social connection, which is essential in Chinese social life, is the way to get things done. Therefore, instead of taking the official avenue, I tried using my connections in gaining access to a field site. I was accepted as a researcher by the school officials of Central High School, who were enthusiastic about educational research projects.

Although Central High School enrolls students ranging from 7th grade to 12th grade, this study focuses on the 10th, 11th, and 12th graders. The majority of the 10th, 11th, and 12th graders are between the ages of 15 and 18, born between July 1, 1979 and July 1, 1982. According to the questionnaire, 11 percent of them are 15 years old; 43 percent of them are 16 years old; 33 percent of them are 17 years old; and 13 percent of them are 18 years.

According to Piaget (1932), children over 11 years old start to move into the stage of formal operations from the stage of concrete operations in their cognitive development (Smith, Cowie, and Blades 1998). As this study reveals, the majority of 10th, 11th and 12th graders at Central High School were able to respond to interview questions with logical reasoning and theoretical thinking.

In addition, according to Kohlberg's (1969) stage theory, the moral development of students between the ages of 16 and 18 is at the conventional level and their moral reasoning is largely based on socially shared systems of moral rules, roles and norms. They identify themselves not only with their family or small community, but also with the society as a whole. They make moral judgments in reference to legal, social, and moral institutions and systems of beliefs (Figurski 2000). Ma (1988) suggests that cultural elements do not affect Chinese youth at the conventional stage. It is reasonable to believe that these students' responses will help shed light on the understanding of the complicity of Chinese society and its influences on the students.

Moral education in China is such a broad and complicated topic that delimitation and limitation of this study become very important. As Lee (1996) suggests, Chinese moral education involves many aspects and it can be studied at various levels, such as the level of debate and discourse, the level of implementation, and the level of government policies. Also, studies done at different levels on different aspects may generate quite diverse discoveries.

This study is basically an attitudinal study. It investigates student's attitudes toward the moral education curriculum taught at a particular school. Although some parents, teachers, and administrators are informally interviewed, this study is primarily based on students' interview and questionnaire data. Thus, this study only reflects the students' attitudes and their perceptions of the moral education curriculum, which may not be in harmony with that of the teachers, administrators, parents, and the government found in other studies.

Moreover, students' attitudes toward the moral education curriculum as revealed in this study should be evaluated with caution. As Perlmutter and Shapiro (1987) suggest, adults and adolescents have deep, heartfelt, and oftentimes conflicting opinions on the establishment of moral codes and values. Due to their developmental characteristics, it is typical for tenth, eleventh, and twelfth graders to rebel against tradition and authority. It is likely that some students in this study may overstate their negative feelings.

In addition, this study does not intend to discuss areas beyond the moral education curriculum as taught at Central High School. Given the variety and the geographically unbalanced development of Chinese secondary school education, it is impossible for a single research study to capture the complete picture of Chinese secondary school moral education. The current study limits itself to Central High School, a small part of a much larger picture. It seeks to draw a small but authentic portrait of moral education in an urban state-run secondary school in Southwestern China. It is believed that "fittingness" (Guba and Lincoln 1981, 1982) rather than classical generalizability is a better criterion for the validity of this study. Therefore, this study strives to provide a detailed description of Central High School and its political and social surroundings, which will help determine whether its conclusions may be useful in understanding other sites.

According to Bronfenbrenner's (1979) ecological theory, multiple environmental factors may influence school moral education practice. These factors may include the overarching ideology and belief system of the society, institutions and organizations, parents' work places, home and school, as well as the interplay of all these environmental factors. The current study is not able to discuss all these factors. Instead, it focuses on basic elements within the school setting, pragmatic ideology, economic policy change, and media impact, which are believed to be most influential in shaping students' attitudes toward the moral education curriculum.

## Organization of the Book

The current study is divided into seven chapters. The first chapter is an introduction. Chapter 2 reviews previous studies on moral education, focusing on the strengths and drawbacks of the theories and approaches applied in these studies. Chapter 3 discusses research methodology. It validates the method of combining qualitative and quantitative research in this study. It also describes the process of data collection and data analysis. Chapter 4 provides background information for this study. It offers demographic information as well as a detailed description of the moral education curriculum at Central High School. Chapter 5 presents findings about students' attitudes toward the moral education curriculum. Chapter 6 discusses the environmental factors that contribute to students' attitudes toward the moral education curriculum. Chapter 7 summarizes the study and provides suggestions and recommendations.

# 2

## LITERATURE REVIEW

There has been a resurgence of scholarly interest in Chinese moral education in the West as well as within China, especially after the student democratic movement in 1989. Chinese moral education is a complicated topic. It involves many aspects and can be studied at various levels (Lee 1996). At the level of debate and discourse, there exists an abundance of literature published in the form of journal articles or books; at the level of implementation, researchers have conducted studies on individual schools; at the level of the state, policy documents are examined. Studies done at different levels on different aspects may generate quite diverse discoveries.

In this chapter, literature related to the field of Chinese moral education will be reviewed. First, the Chinese theory of moral learning will be examined in comparison with prevalent Western moral theories. Second, major studies on contemporary Chinese moral education conducted by both Western scholars and Chinese scholars will be considered. These studies cover the principles, content and practice of moral education in China. Third, studies on Chinese students' attitudes toward moral education will be reviewed. Both Western and Chinese researchers have contributed to our understanding of Chinese students' responses to moral education and the impact of social changes on these responses. Finally, the strengths and drawbacks of the studies in the field of Chinese moral education will be summarized and the contribution of the current study will be presented.

## Theoretical Issues of Moral Education

Theories of moral learning can be grouped into three main camps: social learning theories, psychoanalytical theories and cognitive theories (Nunner-Winkler 1994). Each of them places a different emphasis on the three aspects of morality: behavior, motivation and judgment. Social learning theories focus on moral behavior; psychoanalytical theories focus on moral motivation; and cognitive theories focus on moral judgment. Each approach differs from the other in their methodology and in their basic assumptions concerning human nature and learning mechanisms.

Social learning theories focus on moral behavior and explain it in terms of conditioning and modeling while giving little consideration to subjects' intentions and contextualized moral judgments. Psychoanalytic theories emphasize motivation as the primary mechanism in moral reasoning, suggesting that moral behavior and evaluation are determined by an incorporation of societal norms represented by parents. Both approaches have been criticized for identifying moral norms with existing norms and considering individuals as passive subjects in socialization (Nunner-Winkler 1994).

Figurski (2000) suggests that research on moral development over the past 45 years has focused primarily on the development of moral judgment due to the influence of Lawrence Kohlberg (1969, 1971, 1976) and Jean Piaget (1932).

Nunner-Winkler (1994) suggests that Piaget (1932) identified two stages of moral reasoning in children: heteronymous morality and autonomous morality. During the first stage, children make moral judgments according to consequences and see rules as absolute. During the second stage, they begin to see rules as an instrument for human purpose and make moral judgments based on intention. Seen from a cognitive perspective, children are active agents constantly trying to make sense of the world by reconstructing the rules in a process of reasoning. Cognitive theories are generally believed to be more adequate for describing moral development (Nunner -Winkler 1994).

According to Figurski (2000), Kohlberg (1969, 1971, 1976) expands Piaget's (1932)'s model beyond childhood. Kohlberg hypothesized a sequence of six special stages of moral judgment in individual development, from pre-conventional egocentrism (stages 1 and 2) to conventional egocentrism (stages 3 and 4) to post-conventional conceptions of fairness and justice (stages 5 and 6). Kohlberg suggested that at the highest level, a person follows self-chosen ethical principles, which are equality of human rights and respect for the dignity of human beings as individual persons, even when laws violate these principles.

Kohlberg (1969, 1971, 1976) believes that there is a set of universal values and the six stages of development are universally applicable. His claim of universal validity for his stage theory has become controversial. Kohlberg has been accused of ethnocentrism (Simpson 1974) and gender bias (Gilligan 1982). It is argued that stage theory defines and measures morality in ways that favor American males over other groups.

There are empirical data suggesting that there are two kinds of morality (Triandis 1989). Morality is viewed differently in collective and individualistic cultures. Morality in a collective culture is considered more absolute, more contextual, and depends more on one's status in the society than in an individualistic culture. Empirical studies have found the presence of stages 1–4 in diverse cultures, yet post-conventional thinking is only found in urban male populations, not in traditional tribal and village populations in either Western or non-Western societies (Snarey 1985).

Ma (1988) examined Kohlberg's (1976, 1981) stage theory in the Chinese context. Ma suggested that while the first three stages can be considered universal, the last three stages have cultural elements. Therefore, Ma followed Kohlberg's model for stages 1–3, but presented his own version of stages 4–6. During stage 4, the Chinese perspective on morality is more collectivistic and affective, more tolerant of compromise, more human-centered and less institutionalized compared with its Western counterpart. During stage 5, the Chinese perspective stresses a natural, autonomous, affective, and self-sacrificing altruistic disposition, whereas in the West the emphasis is on the greater good for the majority. During stage 6, the Chinese perspective focuses on living in harmony with nature, having few desires and being less judgmental while the Western view emphasizes equal rights and freedom to chose one's own principles (Triandis 1989).

Walker and Moran (1991) conducted an empirical study on moral reasoning in Communist China. They found that some indigenous concepts, fundamental to moral reasoning in Communist China could not be measured by Kohlberg's (1981,1984) stage theory.

For instance, the Chinese subjects showed a strong reluctance to generalize moral principles from concrete situations. Instead, they argued for a "concrete analysis of a concrete situation" (Walker and Moran 1991:153).

It is not hard to understand why the cognitive approach has had little impact on moral education in China despite its great influence in the West. Cognitive theories focus on the structure and process of moral reasoning instead of the content of morality or specific rights and wrongs. The cognitive approach, therefore, is not considered suitable for encouraging collective morality in China's collective culture. As Ban (1999) noted, although Kohlberg (1984) made a breakthrough in his understanding of children as moral philosophers, his theory is greatly flawed because it neglects the aspects of affection and behavior, which are central to the Chinese approach to moral education.

It is fair to say that the Chinese approach to moral education falls within the camp of social learning theories. In contemporary China, as well as in Confucian China, moral learning has always heavily relied on indoctrination through modeling and imitation, which is central to moral socialization theory (Bakken 1991). Such a tradition can be traced back to the Confucian understanding of human development.

According to H. Lin (1988) Confucianism holds that people are born inclined to virtuous thoughts and actions. The core of Confucian virtue is *ren*, benevolence or human-heartedness. As a process, *ren* represents the way to establish reasonable, harmonious interaction with others. Therefore, moral learning in Confucianism is intended to actualize one's heaven-endowed virtue through self-cultivation and social relationships.

Although Confucian theory of moral development is not a stage theory, Confucius (551–479 BC) in *The Great Learning* postulated a "hierarchy of learning foci" (H. Lin 1988:125). Social order and peace were achieved by a sequence of steps beginning with the individual, extending to one's family, reaching out to the community, and eventually encompassing the world. Tran (1991) suggested that the confusion between means and ends, and the ambiguity in the sequence from the individual to the state and back to the individual in Confucius' teaching proved beneficial to the state. After Confucius, morality became the most important if not the only way of governing in China.

It is obvious that the Confucian moral learning theory is similar to Durkheim's (1973) model of moral socialization. Durkheim directed his attention to the process of socialization, whereby a person learns what to think and feel and what to do, through instruction and explanation, role models, and group reinforcement (Bakken 2000). From a moral socialization perspective, moral education is primarily about social solidarity, group conformity, and mutual support; collective responsibility is considered central to promoting moral character in the classroom as well as in the

*(handwritten margin note: Confucian ideas)*

larger society; and indoctrination is believed to be an effective means to teach pro-social moral values and behavior (Snarey 1992).

The radical changes occurring in contemporary Chinese society, such as the disillusionment with Communist ideology and the intrusion of Western ideas, have created challenges to the traditional model of moral education. Researchers and educators as well as policymakers have been searching for new models of moral education. The affection model (Zhu 1996, 2000) and activity model (Qi 1995, 1999) seek to increase the effectiveness of inculcating the desired moral values among youngsters by appealing to their emotions and engaging them in activities. Another important model is the curriculum model (Wei 1995). It seeks to reinforce moral teaching through the establishment of a grand curriculum system that includes explicit and hidden curriculum, and formal and informal curriculum within the school and beyond.

The newest trend in scholarly discussions in the field of moral education concerns the value of individuals. Many Chinese scholars argue that traditional indoctrination in moral education is no longer appropriate for the new economic order, which requires risk-takers with greater initiative and independence. Therefore, these scholars call for a more student-centered approach in moral education.

Ban (2001) advocated liberating moral education in order to encourage creativity among students. He argued that, to liberate the creative potential of students, it is necessary for moral education to foster a democratic, harmonious and cooperative teacher-student relationship, a friendly and tolerant classroom atmosphere, and lively and diverse teaching methods.

Scholarly discussions have also taken up the topics of subject-orientation (Sun, Cheng, Zhu, Tian, Huang, and Chen 1995; Zhang 2000) and enjoyment function of moral education (J. Lu 1995). However, discussions concerning the value of the individual are largely limited to pragmatic concerns such as the current economy and party line (Meyer 1990) rather than leading to a "deepened concept of the value of individual, some more elemental revelation of the person who transcends the contemporary situation" (p. 22).

In addition, these scholarly discussions remain at the level of theoretical reflection. There is still a large gap between the theories and their implementation. It is fair to say that the approach to moral education in contemporary China is still traditional indoctrination, which is central to social learning theories.

## Development of Chinese Moral Education

It is a widely accepted notion that moral education in China is highly integrated with politics. According to Tran (1991), after Confucius, morality became the most important, if not the only, way to govern. Chinese culture became a moral culture and Chinese politics became "the moral art of governing" (p. 116). Morality became the cornerstone of politics.

Confucius describes eight steps of moral learning: investigating things, extending knowledge, sincerity of will, correction of the mind, cultivation of one's personal life, ruling one's family, national order and world peace (Tran 1991). According to Tran, however, this does not establish whether moral conduct is for the sake of the state or the world; rather, morality is the best means for both. "The confusion of means and ends, and the ambiguity in the sequence from individual to the state, and back to the individual, were used extensively in favor of the State" (p. 117).

Moral education, whether in traditional China or Communist China, has always been highly integrated with the politics of the regimes (Yuan 2001). As in Taiwan, moral education has been transformed from a noble course for man into an instrument for transmitting ideological and political values (Tran 1991). As a result moral education in China has a strong political connotation.

In China, moral education is sometimes called ideological education or political education, and moral quality is sometimes called ideological-moral qualities. These terms are interchangeably used in the literature, and they are conceptually intertwined with one another. The connotation of the term also suggests that moral education is directive in nature; that is, it has been seen by the central government as a means of transmitting ideological and political values. (Lee 1996:5)

Moral education in China has always been a means of serving the agenda of the regime in power (M. Li 1990; Meyer 1990; Price 1992). In Mao's China, moral education served political struggle especially during the Cultural Revolution. During the reform period, as the focus of the CCP's work changed from political struggle to economic development, moral education has been adapted to serve the needs of the new era. Meyer (1990) confirmed that moral education in the reform period is not intended for individual development but for nation building.

Although Chinese educators, scholars and officials recently raised the question of the value of individuality in moral education, such a discussion was limited to concerns of economic development and the Party line. Now the new economic order requires individuals with initiative, enterprise, self-respect and self-confidence, people willing to take risks and responsibilities. It is believed that moral education must change to stimulate the formation of persons who can build the new economy (Meyer 1990).

Meyer (1990) believed that moral education in the reform period is simply seen as the agent of socialist reconstruction during this era. However, although Marxist ideology has been downplayed in the reform period, it is wrong to believe that the Chinese authorities also intended to downplay the role of moral education. Despite the more pragmatic framework that has existed during this period, Price (1992) presented evidence that China's leaders have intensified moral and political control in order to prevent students from drifting away from traditional communist ideals. The Chinese authorities have exhibited strong support for moral/political teaching during the reform era. New organizations such as *Qingnian Sixiang Jiaoyu Yanjiu Zhongxin* (the Youth Ideological-Political Education Research Center) were established during this period.

Bakken (2000) pointed out that China's reform program is a controlled program and that the government has emphasized moral education in order to offset the side effects of the reform program. Moral education is intended to help promote the CCP ideology and solidarity in Chinese society, which are regarded as pre-requisites for accomplishing the reform program. It is a widely accepted notion that the Party always wants to control ideological and political life in China (Bakken 2000; Thogerson 1990; Tu 1994).

In fact, the influence of the Party's old control mechanisms endures to this day and China is still very much controlled by official ideology (Bakken 2000; Reed 1995b). While acknowledging the increasing challenges brought about by societal changes, Reed stated that the necessity and efficacy of moral/political education are unquestioned and pedagogies for its implementation have been fine-tuned through the centuries.

Reed (1995) took a comparative approach to look at the formation and implementation of moral education policy in China and in the United States. Reed believed that the formation and implementation of moral education policy in China are less problematic than in the United States. He examined the set of underlying beliefs and values in China's socio-political system that contributed to this phenomenon. Unlike America, where the teaching of moral ethics, values or character development can be seen as a threat to the constitutional separation between church and state, in China it is a legitimate role of the government to provide moral/political guidance to the populace. This is largely because both Confucianism and socialism are human-centered systems that reject religious belief and practice.

*Similar to, but separate from, religious ideology and ideology.*

In addition, free from the influence of scientific objectivism in the West, there is a notion of inseparability of fact and value in the Chinese epistemology. Any piece of information has value, and especially under the regime of the CCP, knowledge benefits the people, the Party, and further, the socialist good. Also, the Chinese are not particularly interested in truth and falsity in the Greek sense when encountering a belief or proposition. What matters to the Chinese are the practical implications of such a belief or proposition. Reed believed that this largely explains the different responses to the story of the Communist model Lei Feng in America and in China (1995b). While Americans may see Lei Feng as a political fabrication of no consequence, for the Chinese, believing in and following Lei Feng's example was not only politically correct but also resulted in more virtuous people and a more harmonious society.

Reed (1995b) also suggested that, unlike in America, where autonomy and individual rights are highly valued, in China the individual is defined in social terms in both Confucian and socialist thought. Therefore, there is less tension between individualism and commitment to the community in China than in America. The transmission of societal beliefs and values through codes of morality and rules for social interaction is unquestioned in China.

As Reed (1995b) has reminded us, however, it is important to note that long-held beliefs and embedded values have begun to change in the emerging Chinese society and have undermined the tradition of moral education. Recent changes in China have made moral education increasingly problematic. For instance, disillusionment with the CCP and the rethinking of the relationship between the individual and the state has created challenges to the legitimacy and primacy of Chinese moral education.

Chinese moral education during the reform era has undergone considerable changes in policy. Lee (1996) conducted a study on moral education policy, examining the shifts of emphasis in the various educational documents during the reform era. Lee suggested that changes in moral education policy mirrored the changes in the political and ideological arena at the time and reflected the government's "ideopolitical stand" (Lee 1996:11).

Lee (1996) suggested that educational documents written during 1978–1979 clearly pointed to the destruction of the Cultural Revolution and the need for respecting knowledge and talents. Both political orientation and professional expertise were stressed.

During the period of 1980–1982, moral education documents emphasized the importance of expertise for the realization of socialist modernization in accordance with reform initiatives. A civil courtesy campaign, the five stresses and four beauties campaign was launched for the construction of a socialist spiritual civilization. Ideological work was regarded as a means of upholding socialist and communist thought that met the needs of a new era (Lee 1996).

During 1983–1984, in an effort to counteract anti-spiritual influences, directives on strengthening moral and ideological work were issued. Documents during this period called for patriotic education to halt the decline of patriotism among youth.These documents encouraged the cultivation of students' initiative and applying guidance and persuasion to moral education (Lee 1996).

During 1985–1987, moral education documents mentioned the need to attend to the characteristics of the different stages of students' psychological development. A de-politicized tone could be identified in these documents. However, a tension could be noted between the calls for upholding the Four Cardinal Principles and the calls for openness and independent thinking (Lee 1996).

During the period of 1988–1989, moral education documents clearly expressed the need for policies that emphasized openness and student initiative. The documents called for building a democratic, peer-directed, and harmonious classroom atmosphere in the teaching of moral education; developing capacities of independent thinking, autonomy, and self-education; and establishing a principal-responsibility system, which signified further decentralization and liberation in moral education (Lee 1996).

In 1990 and beyond, moral education documents seemed to continue the previous emphasis on openness with a reiteration of the decentralized principal-responsibility system. After the student movement in 1989, a document issued in April 1990 condemned bourgeois liberation and peaceful evolution, but at the same time stressed the need for encouraging student's capacities for self-management and self-education, as well as the integration of collectivism and individualism (Lee 1996).

Lee (1996) concluded that a continuity of student-centered teaching persisted even in an intense time of condemning antisocialist liberation, bourgeois liberation, and peaceful evolution. Despite the "recurrence of the tension between indoctrinary and autonomous orientations" (p. 11), an increasing emphasis on independent thinking and rational teaching can be observed. The trend of openness in moral education also included the policies of the principal-responsibility system and the regionalization of curriculum development.

Lee's (1996) examination of the policy documents discloses the shifts in emphasis in the Chinese government's moral education policy. However, this study is limited in that there is always a gap between policy and its implementation. Other studies reveal that it has become increasingly difficult for government policy to be implemented as intended at the local school level during the reform period.

Cheng Kai-ming (1995), a prominent scholar of Chinese education, argued that decentralization of education reform has weakened the link between the central government and local schools. Local schools have more autonomy as well as financial responsibilities. At the secondary school level, the state only pays teachers' salaries; all other expenses must be borne by the local government and community. As a result of this enormous financial burden schools have become profit-driven (Ross 1991).

As Tu (1994), a well-known scholar in Chinese studies, suggested, there is a tendency in China for people to give priority to their small collective (to whom they owe secondary loyalty) over the Party (to whom they owe first loyalty). Many local officials pay lip service to the slogans that come from the government and lobby the government for resources, but they do not carry out official directives faithfully (Lieberthal 1995). Chan (1997) found in her study of a secondary school in Shanghai that the principal applied official policies inconsistently and that he bent the policies to meet the different expectations of the parents, the school staff, and the school district officials.

Besides the shifting policies of moral education, textbooks for political courses have undergone changes. J. Lin (1993) conducted a content analysis of the textbooks used for political studies as well as language arts and history courses at the primary and secondary level. Most of these textbooks were published in 1998 and 1989. J. Lin discovered that the content emphasis and editorial styles of the textbooks changed during the reform period, which she believes were a reflection of the political and social changes caused by the reform policies.

Political study courses, which are required to be taken by all students in Post-Mao China, are broader in scope than other academic courses. These courses used to typically include Marxist philosophy, political economy, the history of the Chinese Communist Party, and the history of the world Communist movement. New courses such as citizenship education, ethics education, social history and common knowledge of socialist reconstruction have been added (J. Lin 1993).

The major concern of citizenship education and ethics education is the development of desirable attitudes and behaviors toward the Communist authorities and government, as well as toward the general public and individual self. The common knowledge of socialist reconstruction textbook helps the students understand the current economic reforms in China. The textbooks use theoretical justification and practical examples to teach the students that China must maintain a socialist system with Chinese Characteristics. They also introduce the students to China's legal system and instruct the students about their rights and duties. One of these duties is to embrace the Four Cardinal Principles (J. Lin 1993).

Besides the changes in content emphasis, the editorial style of the textbooks has been modified to reflect a child's developmental characteristics. For example, illustrations and photographs have been added. The language is less politicized, even neutral, with a thematic shift from class struggle to economic reconstruction (J. Lin 1993).

Thogerson (1990) indicated that in the teaching outline for political courses published in 1981, the subjects taught in the junior section are listed as the moral self-cultivation of young people, general knowledge of the law, and brief history of social development; for the senior section, the listed subjects are political economy and dialectic materialism. The stated aim of these political courses is to instruct students on both the Chinese version of socialist morality and the CCP's propaganda on Marxist theory and contemporary political issues.

Price (1992) and Meyer (1990) both conducted content analyses of political studies textbooks used in primary and secondary schools. Despite modifications to the textbooks, the researchers conclude that the textbooks are still problematic. Specifically, they found that the textbooks used to teach moral education neglect to take into account the characteristics of students' cognitive development. For example, the level of abstraction in the textbooks is too high and there is a lack of sufficient concrete materials for the students to comprehend the abstract concepts.

The prevailing political line has altered the balance in curriculum between political study and the learning of skills and scientific knowledge. During the reform period, there has been a shift from "virtuocracy" to "meritocracy" as defined by Shirk (1982:4). Political courses no longer dominate the school curriculum and the schools have shifted their focus to academic subjects. In present day China, political study is again confined to a narrow part of the curriculum, in the interest of giving students education that will help advance China's modernization (Ogden 2002).

One of the major characteristics of Chinese moral education is what Meyer called "pervasiveness" (Meyer 1990:6). Besides courses explicitly teaching morality/ideology, the entire school curriculum and extra-curricular activities are expected to contribute to the moral formation of the students. Reed suggested that the phrase "Chinese moral education" was not an "oxymoron," but rather a "redundancy" (1995b:248), by which he means that, traditionally, all education in China was seen as having a moral/political dimension.

Language arts, history, and geography instructional materials contain moral messages. J. Lin (1993) noted that, instead of being limited to teaching students how to read and write, Chinese language textbooks use stories, poems, fables, pictures, and the like, to pass on cultural values, to teach certain habits, and to inculcate political values and beliefs. The same emphasis on patriotism and selflessness is found in the primary and secondary school textbooks used for political and language arts courses (Meyer 1990).

In addition, Thogerson (1990) suggested that moral values are implanted through the entire school system. Typical manifestations of the operation of these moral values are the regulations and behavior standards for middle school students and the five stresses and four beauties campaign.

According to Thogerson (1990), the rules for secondary students combine general and rather abstract principles with down-to-earth rules of behavior, while the daily behavior standards for middle school students describe in more detail how middle school students should behave. These standards promote "the ideal image of the well-behaved, modest, obedient, well-adapted middle school student of the 1950s. They show no trace of influence from the reform ideas about the need for a more vigorous, independent-minded young generation" (p. 123).

The five stresses and four beauties campaign has been the most important ideological education campaign to take place during the reform period. Its content can be summed up in a few cardinal virtues: selflessness, collectivism and patriotism, discipline, obedience, frugality and a simple lifestyle (Thogerson 1990).

Many scholars have noted that the content of moral education in Chinese schools is a combination of traditional Confucian values, patriotism and socialist principles (Price 1992; Reed 1995b; Thogerson 1990). Moral training in Chinese middle schools encourages the subordination of individual interests to the interests of the group, the family and the nation (Thogerson 1990).

Patriotism has become the most important theme in moral education in recent years. With the decline of Marxist ideology, China's leaders seem to be relying on patriotism and nationalism as the key components of a new ideology whose primary purpose is very simple: economic modernization and support of the CCP leadership (Ogden 2002). Tu has pointed out that under the banner of patriotism, the Chinese government is making every effort to maintain the status quo. Confucianism and capitalism are used to prop up the socialist flag. Traditional symbols are employed to promote nationalism and a market economy is used to prop up the flag of socialism with Chinese Characteristics (1994).

The methods used to implant moral values among Chinese youth have not changed since the 1950s, and modeling, rewards, and sanctions are still dominant (Bakken 1991; Thogerson 1990). Price (1992) found that the teaching methods in moral/political courses in Chinese secondary schools are mainly rote learning and recitation. Critical analysis is not taught in these courses because it is believed a high level of abstraction is beyond students' understanding.

Many scholars (Bakken 1991; Z. Li 1995; Reed 1991) suggested that in traditional pedagogical practices the use of role models as a means to socialize young children in Chinese schools has been a powerful tool for centuries. Reed (1991) argued that the set of core virtues that Chinese school children are learning from Lei Feng's example, such as loyalty, filial piety, self-cultivation through education, benevolence, modesty and frugality, have roots in the Confucian tradition.

The government has launched educational campaigns using the Communist model, Lei Feng several times since the 1960s. Despite significant differences, the virtues that were being cultivated by learning from Lei Feng's example were essentially the same as the virtues that were cultivated through the emulation of traditional Confucian models. Reed considered Lei Feng a "proletarianised version of earlier Confusion prototypes" (1991:105). Lei Feng's ultimate loyalty was directed toward Chairman Mao, the Party and the people. Lei Feng was an orphan yet he was the "most filial of all sons" in the "big socialist family" (p. 107). The primary textbook for Lei Feng's self-cultivation is Mao's writings. Benevolence or human-heartedness, the essence of Lei Feng's spirit, is also the highest virtue of the Confucian role model.

However, as Bakken (1991) pointed out, efforts to modernize old methods in present-day China have created a paradox. The traditional method of imitating and emulating models has certainly met with new difficulties during the reform period. In discussing the modernization of personality, some scholars have suggested that the modern person should have "a strong concept of time," "an enterprising spirit," and qualities such as "effectiveness," "scientific knowledge," "reason," "optimism," and "a unique individual character" (p. 131). Bakken (1991) agreed with Yu Wujin, a Chinese scholar, who pointed out that those who criticize the old culture are themselves products of this tradition and tend to identify with the tradition. Therefore, the modernizing of old methods is a paradoxical process.

Some scholars (J. Lin 1993; Thogerson 1990) noted that social reality in China largely contradicts the teachings at school. This contradiction causes confusion among the students and discredits the moral teaching at school (Thogerson 1990). J. Lin (1993) suggested that the great disparity between the reality the students experience in society and what is taught at school makes the indoctrination less effective. For example, government corruption, which has become severe during the reform period, is barely mentioned in textbooks. The confusion and doubts that people have about Communist ideology, distrust of the CCP, and public dissatisfaction with the government are not addressed in these texts.

Thogerson (1990) suggested that the values transmitted through moral education have been contradicted not only by the surrounding society, but also more specifically by the hidden curriculum of the schools themselves. This has created difficulties for those students who really want to live up to the publicly sponsored ideals. For example, selflessness is hard to practice within the competitive education system and under the massive propaganda campaign against egalitarianism.

Hypocrisy is not a specifically Chinese phenomenon, but the combination of very mixed ideological signals in the media as well as in school (selflessness and competitiveness both being preached at the same time), and an obvious lack of moral quality in the leadership have made the well-known "do as I say, not as I do" trick very difficult to perform convincingly. (p. 125)

In addition, the virtues of obedience and discipline are rewarded in the school system. But the teacher-centered teaching method does not encourage initiative and independent thinking by students. On the other hand, the universities and society have called for more risk-taking and inventive students.

Also, the virtue of a simple lifestyle has been challenged by the development of Chinese consumerism. The love of labor is discouraged by an exam-oriented education system in which the students focus on their academic studies instead of doing housework and other manual jobs.

It is a widely accepted notion that moral education in Chinese schools has not achieved its stated goal, which can be summarized as transforming students' moral framework into a socialist framework. The Chinese government has recognized the problem, as Deng openly admitted in 1989 that the worst omission of the past ten years was in education, particularly in political education (Meyer 1990).

Ross (1991) suggested that although both teachers and CCP officials agree that schools have not been successful in inculcating moral values among students, they differ as to the reasons behind the failure. The teachers blamed reform policies, which they believed caused the students to be disinterested in the teaching of moral values. The officials believed that the teachers did not provide enough ideological guidance for the students.

Meyer (1990) quoted the Assistant Director of China National Education Committee, who described several problems troubling those engaged in the work of moral education. These included an excessive emphasis on examinations and inadequate preparation of moral education teachers. Meyer also added five other problems based on his own study.

I would like to add to the list five other problems which were frequently mentioned in my talks with educators: (1) the bad influence of society, media, resulting in uncivilized behavior and money worship, (2) the low level of teachers salaries, (3) a big gap between the high ideals taught in school and the reality of current social life, (4) current students lack of interest in ideology, and (5) a very traditional classroom method which is too tied to the textbooks. (1990:19)

Scholars in the West and in China share a common belief as to the most important factor contributing to the so-called ineffectiveness of Chinese moral education: The old methods of political education were no longer effective when Chinese youth became skeptical of both traditional and communist morality. This skepticism developed among students because of the contradictory nature of Marxism, socialism and communism (Meyer 1990).

Rosen (1991) observed that in addition to the skepticism of students, political work cadres had become demoralized. A majority of the political workers in universities in Beijing wanted to change their profession.

Chan (1997) suggested in her study of a Chinese secondary school that the school failed to transform the students' moral framework into the desired socialist moral framework. Chan believed that the main reason for this failure was the school's pragmatic moral education strategy. In order to meet the different expectations of the state, parents, and teachers, the principal applied a "situational poetics" strategy that muddied the moral values to be taught to the students. As a result of this process moral education became discredited among the students.

## Qualitative Approach to Chinese Moral Education

Among the different voices in the debate on moral education, the voice of the students is very faint. It is obvious that Chinese students dislike moral education, especially the traditional indoctrination methods and the political courses. However, there is little research devoted to a more comprehensive understanding of moral education from a student perspective.

According to Perlmutter and Shapiro (1987) adolescence is a time of extraordinarily intense and visible dramatic changes in all areas of a growing child's life.

At the center of these changes, the adolescent is attempting to determine a unique sense of self within relationships to family, community of peers, and the larger society. Their exploration of unique morals and values is often regarded as the hallmark of adolescent development. (p. 187)

Perlmutter and Shapiro (1987) cited Elder (1975) and Riley (1976) that the development of adolescent morals and values should be examined in light of the social forces that operate during a particular historical period and that the social climate influences adolescent morals and values through historical time. They also suggested, while the youth culture in America during the 1960s and the 1970s stressed rejection of parental values and socially accepted traditions, the generation of the 1980s was more practical, more interested in financial security, and perhaps less moral than their predecessors.

In a similar fashion, the youth culture in China in the past decades has undergone significant changes within the social transformation that is taking place in Chinese society. During the 1980s in China, a youth culture began to appear, representing a lifestyle very different from that of the traditional communist model, largely due to exposure to Western lifestyles through the media, such as films, magazines and television (Thogerson 1990).

Thogerson (1990) noted that the CCP leadership has paid close attention to changes in students' ideology since 1980, when they realized that economic reforms influenced young people's thinking in a number of unpredictable and undesired ways, and they have sponsored many surveys on youth problems. The low moral quality of the students of the 1980s is reported in these surveys. Students have been accused of being selfish, being uninterested in politics and in the future of their country, looking down on manual labor, wasting their time on love affairs and their money on drinking and eating out.

Chin's (1988) book, *Children of China,* is one of the few qualitative studies focusing on the attitudes of Chinese middle school students. Chin conducted interviews with students and found that students in post-Mao China are more independent in mind and spirit.

Rosen (1989, 1994) conducted a review of Chinese studies surveying changes in values among students under the impact of economic reform. He found that the values of youth in the 1980s were very different from those of their counterparts in the 1950s, 1960s, and 1970s. According to Rosen, Chinese youth have become more independent in their thinking, skeptical of both traditional and Communist morality, and resistant to collective values. For example, "political commitments and unquestioning loyalty toward the CCP have declined at the expense of independence of thought and judgment, respect for talent, and a patriotism separated from party leadership" (1989: 200–201).

Based on his examination of more recent surveys conducted after the student movement in 1989 Rosen (1994) noted that the attitudes and behavior of youth in the 1990s are merely a continuation of the same trends in the 1980s. Empirical data compiled by Rosen during his review revealed that the decline of regime-sponsored values was more extensive, the level of discontent higher, and individualism among youth more prevalent.

Besides their skepticism of the political model, there is a more serious trend of malaise among university students in the 1990s. It is said that the new slogan of university students is "it doesn't matter" (Rosen 1994:2) and the students are blamed for lacking a sense of responsibility (Rosen 1994).

According to Rosen (1994), a review of longitudinal studies revealed that in the 1990s there were changes in fundamental values among youth. The emphasis on gaining material benefits at the expense of commonly accepted values has increased. Money was becoming the most important factor in choosing a job. Also, students over the five-year period had become more willing to compete for scarce resources like scholarships, with the majority of students now seeing the realization of their self-worth as the ultimate aim of life. The researcher concluded that the values of present day Chinese youth bore a striking resemblance to the Western humanistic philosophy of self-actualization.

Rosen (1994) observed that what is more striking is that these phenomena have filtered down to secondary and primary schools in the 1990s. In middle schools, students seek immediate gratification through activities such as films, television, books, and music from Hong Kong and Taiwan. The traditional activities intended to instill moral education, such as field trips and joining the Communist Youth League [CYL], no longer attract students. Also, consumerism and a lack of appreciation for the value of hard work are common among middle school students.

Survey data also revealed that in primary school there is the same disturbing trend. The majority of elementary students believe in commercialized social relationships. The majority of these students are not interested in the raising of the national flag. In addition, at all levels, corruption is not taken seriously enough (Rosen 1994).

A recent survey noted that self-discipline and the spirit of sacrifice have declined among Chinese students (Zhang and Vaughan 1996). Zhang and Vaughan believed that the students' change of attitudes and behavior are either directly or indirectly the result of the reform program.

Bai (1998) analyzed the surveys of university students' job-selection criteria conducted between 1990 and 1995. He suggested that "money talks" has become a norm guiding social behaviors and personal relationships. In addition, the growth of market forces, translated into "economic efficiency" in the field of education, has undermined the effectiveness of moral education (p. 525).

Confirming the survey findings, a review of Chinese youth magazines disclosed a change in the values of youth between the 1980s and 1990s. Su (1998) observed that youth in the 1980s were reflective on the past of the country, they had a strong commitment to the reform program and the future of the country, and they were interested in political participation. On the other hand, the youth of the 1990s were described as a generation of pragmatism. The youth of the 1990s were focused on materialism, consumerism, and commercialized social relationships.

In a survey of changes in morals and values among the youth in Chengdu, Sichuan conducted in 1997, Tian (1997) found that the young people in Chengdu prefer wealth to morals, individual interest to the collective interest, and taking to giving. According to her, 72 percent of the 600 young people in the study indicated that the meaning of hard work lies in actualizing personal worth and improving one's own standard of living.

Rosen (1994) has suggested that after the student movement in 1989 the Chinese government successfully redirected the interest and energy of young people from politics to economics. Since the conceptualization of market socialism in 1992, the government has officially legitimatized the market as the determining factor in individual choice. This shift in official ideology makes it even more difficult for educators to promote regime values that stress collectivism.

The majority of the above studies on Chinese youth are survey studies. It is believed that qualitative studies on youth attitudes and values are crucial in this field. A qualitative approach can offer deeper insights into the attitudes and values of students in the intimate setting in which they live their lives. Therefore, the current study attempts to understand Chinese youth in the late 1990s through interviews and observations. It seeks to analyze their attitudes towards moral education, which are believed to be a reflection of their morals and values.

Western literature on political and moral education in secondary schools in contemporary China are largely analyses of policies or textbooks that were drafted prior to China's opening up to the outside world. Shirk (1982) had to base her studies on interviews of refugees in Hong Kong.

Greater openness and improved conditions for doing social research in China have led to an increasing number of ethnographic studies of Chinese secondary schools. Although moral education may not be their major area of concern, some of these studies (Ross 1993; Schoenhals 1993) have contributed to our understanding of the implementation of moral education in secondary schools during the reform era.

Ross (1993) conducted an ethnographic study in a language school in Shanghai. Her analysis of the teaching and learning methods at the school revealed a hierarchical system and a controlled school culture and the restraints they placed on the lives of the teachers and their students. At the same time, she described how this school conducted moral education. Through school rules, formal student organizations, and numerous political campaigns, this school compelled the students to think and act in a prescribed manner and conform to national political values.

Ross (1993) observed a discrepancy between the stated educational policy and the tacit knowledge and practices of many teachers and their students at this school. It appeared that schooling was "the enactment of a carefully written script" (p. 15) emulating a predefined model of excellence. At the same time, the teachers practiced an "eclecticism" (p. 103) that allowed them to bend the official policy to fit their pedagogical needs. Also, the teachers as well as their students utilized their "dialectic wits" and became "finely balanced weather vanes" to protect themselves in the fast-changing political campaigns (p. 167). Ross' imagery of this school as a theater provided a useful analogy for understanding the culture of Chinese secondary schools.

Schoenhals (1993) conducted an ethnographic study of an elite secondary school, Third Affiliated, in northern China. There he studied the balance of power between the teachers and school officials. Schoenhals argued that because face was an essential concept in Chinese culture the teachers at Third Affiliated used face to resist their superiors. He also suggested that face, criticism and evaluation play important roles in educational pedagogy and disciplinary methods in Chinese classrooms. Teachers used public humiliation and the loss of face to discipline their students.

Some ethnographic studies (Chan 1997; Meyer 1990) are exclusively concerned with Chinese secondary school moral education. Meyer (1990) visited 15 elementary and secondary schools of various types in a city near Beijing within a five-month period in 1988–1989. According to Meyer, Chinese moral/political education can be characterized by its pervasiveness, collective morality and systematic treatment. In the secondary schools, moral education fully merged with political indoctrination.

Chan (1997) conducted an ethnographic study on moral education in a regular secondary school in Shanghai. Chan argued that the programmatic moral education in this school failed to transform students' pre-existing moral framework into a socialist framework. It helped keep the students' behavior orderly but it did not change students' decision-making criteria to include consideration of the collective welfare. The major reason for this failure, according to Chan, lay in the fact that those charged with implementation of this policy had to meet the competing expectations of the state, parents, teachers and so on. For example, the state required the cultivation of socialist morality and ideology among the students while parents did not care about it and instead demanded the academic excellence that is needed to prosper in a market-driven economy. In order to fulfill their professional identities, the principal and the teachers had to meet different expectations and thus muddied their endorsement of a socialist moral framework. At the same time, the students were able to conform to different expectations in different situations while preserving their pre-existing moral framework (Chan 1997).

In Chan's study, the imagery of theater (Ross 1993) was applied to moral education. Chan suggested that those involved in moral education were social actors and they employed "situational poetics" (1997:6) to put on different performances for different audiences under different situations. Chan's study shed light on our understanding of the dynamics of programmatic moral education in secondary schools.

Bakken's (2000) investigated the control mechanisms of Chinese schools. Bakken concluded that moral education in China was an instrument of control, achieved through the methods of teaching, evaluation, and discipline. He described Chinese society as an exemplary society in which a set of exemplary norms was established to bring people's behavior into conformity in order to achieve solidarity within the society. Since overt obedient behavior in Chinese society was highly prized, the result was "hypocrisy" and "lies" (p. 411). Everyone became an actor and the entire society became a social theater.

In conclusion, the above ethnographic studies shed light on our understanding of moral education at the level of implementation. These studies suggest that there is a discrepancy between moral education policies and practices in Chinese secondary schools.

It is important to understand Chinese students through their perceptions, opinions and feelings in the environment of their everyday lives as well as through questionnaires. Therefore, it is believed that through a study of students' attitudes toward moral education, we will have a better understanding of the phenomenon of Chinese moral education from the unique perspective of the student. At the same time, it will also help us better comprehend the present student generation, especially their ideology and moral values under the impact of radical social change.

# 3

## METHODOLOGY

This study is about students' attitudes toward moral education curriculum at Central High School (pseudonym) in Southwestern China. It investigates students' attitudes toward the moral education curriculum and the factors that help shape such attitudes at this particular school. This study takes the approach of naturalistic inquiry. It is designed as a case study, which combines qualitative and quantitative research data in order to gain a more complete picture of the students' attitudes toward the moral education curriculum at this school.

### A Qualitative Inquiry

The key words associated with qualitative methods are "complexity, contextual, exploration, discovery, and inductive logic" (Mertens 1998:160). This study seeks to explore the Central High School students' attitudes toward the moral education curriculum in its natural setting. It examines the complexity of the students' attitudes toward the moral education curriculum in the midst of rapid social change. This study focuses on the participant perspective, considering the moral education curriculum from the students' viewpoint in order to illuminate inner dynamics that are often invisible to outsiders. It attempts to describe the students' experience with the moral education curriculum and how they make sense out of that experience through close observations and in-depth interviews.

The case study is considered a type of ethnographic research by many authors while others view it as merely a data collecting method (Mertens 1998). However, both sides agree that the case study "focuses on a special instance (object or case) and reaches an understanding within a complex context" (p. 166). I believe that the case study is a type of qualitative research design rather than a data collecting method. As a research design, the case study can accommodate a variety of data collecting methods. For instance, collecting newspaper articles and other written materials related to the case, conducting interviews and observations as well as surveys can all be applied in case study research.

Using the case study design, this study involves a focused and detailed investigation of students in grades 10 through 12 at Central High School. These students were chosen because they have more experience with the moral education curriculum than students in lower grades. This study covers the period from September 1998 to March 1999, that is, the entire academic semester of fall 1998 and the first months of the academic semester of spring 1999.

Context is pertinent to a case study. Stake (1994) recommends that case study data collection include the nature of the case; its historical background; other contexts, such as economic, political, legal and aesthetic; other cases through which this case is recognized; and those informants through whom the case can be known. This study locates the case within its larger social, political and economic setting. In addition to the students' demographic information, this study describes the social, political and economic environment in which the school is situated in order to better understand how different forces impact the students' experience with the school's moral curriculum.

Another characteristic of the case study lies in the variety of data used in the study. The case study design allows this study to collect and utilize multi-formed data of the case, such as students' writing, photographs and school publications, through a variety of methods, including observation, interview, and questionnaire. This design provides more complete information and enables a better understanding of the students' attitudes toward the moral curriculum at this particular school.

## Integrating Quantitative Data

The paradigm debate challenged the legitimacy of combining quantitative and qualitative data (Reichardt and Cook 1979). Some believe that quantitative data implies the framework of positivism/postpositivism while qualitative data belongs to interpretism/constructivism; therefore the two sets of data are basically incompatible (Guba and Lincoln 1981, 1982). Others point out that there is no reason to tie the distinction to epistemological preferences because the worldview-method argument only creates a fabricated dichotomy (Reichardt and Cook 1979). Some argue that both quantitative and qualitative data are inextricably intertwined at both design and analysis levels (Howe 1985, 1988); therefore, the question is not whether fusion can be accomplished, but whether it should be done, how it should be done, and for what purposes (Miles and Huberman 1994).

Miles and Huberman (1994) review the reasons for combining quantitative and qualitative data. For example, quantitative studies lead to more precise and generalizable results through de-emphasizing individual judgments and stressing established procedures. At the same time, qualitative studies can overcome the abstraction inherent in quantitative studies through rich depictions and strategic comparisons across cases (Firestone 1987). Quantitative data can be used to supply background data and overlooked information and to verify or cast new light on qualitative findings; qualitative data can make access and data collection easier and can validate, interpret, clarify, and illustrate quantitative data (Sieber 1973). In addition, quantitative and qualitative data can confirm each other via triangulation, further elaboration of analysis, and initiation of new lines of thinking from surprises and paradoxes (Rossman and Wilson 1990).

Recent discussion has promoted mixed methods as a distinct research design. Varied models have been developed combining the procedures of quantitative and qualitative methods (Creswell 2002). These models differ from each other in the status of quantitative or qualitative data, the relationship of the two sets of data, and the consequence of the two sets of data in the study.

This case study seeks to build on the strengths of both qualitative and quantitative data. The philosophy underpinning this study is critical realism (Cook and Campbell 1979). It is believed that an objective reality exists but is only imperfectly and probabilistically apprehensible because of flawed human intellectual mechanics. Triangulation of multi-formed data is believed to be the best way to obtain the knowledge that is closest to the truth through examining data collected from different sources or methods. Therefore, this approach combines both questionnaire data as well as in-depth, contextual data in order to gain the best understanding of the students' attitudes toward the moral curriculum at Central High School.

The method of integrating quantitative data with qualitative data in this study follows the mixed method design, in which both quantitative and qualitative data are simultaneously collected, merged, and compared in order to better understand a research problem (Creswell 2002). However, this study does not consider itself a distinct mixed method design; rather, it is basically a qualitative case study, which integrates the questionnaire with qualitative data for a more complete understanding of the research problem.

## Data Collection and Management

The field research for the current study was conducted during a seven-month period from September 1998 to March 1999. I was accepted by Central High School as a researcher in the first week of the 1998 fall semester. I was present at the school every day while classes were in session to do research. During the seven months of field study, participant observation, in-depth interviews, and a questionnaire of students' attitudes were conducted interactively.

Participant observation started on the first day of the field study. I was given a desk and a chair in the political-ideological education department, where I observed the staff planning and supervising moral education work for the entire school. I studied official circulations and school documents as well as other written materials related to moral education collected in the political-ideological education department. I also conducted casual interviews with the staff, who I could relate to due to my previous experience as a high school teacher in China. I attended various activities organized by the department such as field trips, singing contests, and military training.

My role in the political-ideological education department was not that of an onlooker but an active participant. For example, when the local district held an English play competition as part of the nationwide propaganda campaign to promote quality-oriented education, I was entrusted with the task of putting on the play the school would enter into the competition. When the play was awarded a prize in the competition, it helped strengthen my relationship with students, teachers, and school officials who later would lend me greater support for my research.

In addition, from the first day of my field study I was given the opportunity to closely observe a head teacher and her class. I would sit in the back of the classroom watching her conducting moral education as well as observing other teachers addressing moral education while teaching various subjects in this class. I was allowed to read the students' weekly journals in which the students chose whatever they would like to write about as a way of practicing their writing skills. During the few weeks she was absent due to illness I was asked to conduct weekly class meetings and grade the students' weekly journals. I took the opportunity to ask the students to write an essay in their journals about being a moral person. Reading the students' weekly journals greatly helped me in getting to know the students better. By reading their writings about their thoughts, feelings and interests, I began to know them as unique individuals with their own personalities.

I was also asked to do some teaching at Central High School including classes on Spoken English and lecturing on the American school system, teaching methods, and life and culture in America. I took advantage of my teaching assignments to collect data. For example, in my weekly Spoken English class taught to Class Senior 3 (2), I asked the students to discuss in English their ideals, beliefs, and attitudes towards the moral education curriculum. After class I would record in writing the conversations that took place during this class.

At the same time, my teaching and lecturing duties provided me with many opportunities to interact with students, teachers and school officials. Several teachers and students at Central High School became friends of mine. Some teachers invited me out for dinner. I also practiced English with students on the weekends. Many of these students would confide in me.

The students called me "teacher," yet some of them considered me a friend rather than a teacher. At the beginning of the semester some teachers and school officials may have felt that I was a threat or interfering with their jobs, but they later became friendly and supportive. Trust and cooperation were gradually established between my informants at Central High School and me as a researcher.

Besides participant observation and informal interviews, I conducted structured in-depth interviews. After a series of informal interviews, in-depth structured interviews were scheduled and conducted with 21 students chosen from the student population in the senior sector of the school. These students were randomly selected from a list of students. They were from different grades (10th, 11th, and 12th grades) and from different types of classes (slow learners, fast learners, and intermediate). All the selected students but two agreed to be interviewed. Four students were interviewed together as a focus group. The rest of the interviewees were interviewed individually.

In addition to participant observation and in-depth interviews, the students completed a questionnaire. In the middle of conducting the in-depth interviews, a questionnaire was given to the entire student population of the senior sector. The questionnaire had been developed prior to the field study. A pilot study was done with five students who completed the questionnaire. The questionnaire was modified based on feedback from the pilot study and administered to the entire student population of the senior sector.

The questionnaire also benefited from the initial analysis of interview results. Half of the in-depth interviews were conducted before the questionnaire was distributed to the students and therefore provided insights on how to revise some of the questions or obtain necessary information.

The questionnaires were printed at Central High School. The head teachers in each class at the school administered the questionnaire to their students at the same time on a Friday afternoon when they were supposed to hold their weekly class meeting. The completed questionnaires were collected by the head teachers and turned in to me. As a result of the cooperation of the school, especially the supervision by the head teachers, the return rate of the questionnaire was 95 percent. The results of the questionnaire were recorded on a hand-made chart with the help of several assistants and later converted to a SPSS file on the computer for analysis. Interviewees were consulted to clarify some surprising findings after a brief review of the questionnaire answers.

In conclusion, data collection was triangulated in the field study. Participant observation, in-depth interviews, and questionnaires were conducted interactively in the data collecting process. Each procedure informed the other. Participant observations and informal interviews provided information that was used to refine the questionnaire. At the same time, the results of the initial review of the questionnaire data provided guidance for the in-depth interviews and a new focus for participant observation.

## Data Analysis

The quantitative and qualitative data were analyzed interactively. Both sets of data were compared repeatedly during the process of data collection and analysis. Each illuminated and clarified the other. Questionnaire data were used to supply background data and overlooked information and to verify or cast new light on qualitative findings; interview and observation data were used to validate, interpret, clarify, and illustrate questionnaire data. For example, when the questionnaire revealed unexpected or contradictory attitudes of the students, in-depth interviews were used to explore the reasons for the discrepancies; when new themes were extracted from the interview accounts, statistical procedures were utilized to support or reject such findings. Through such triangulation, the convergence, inconsistency and complementary results of this study were identified and reported to provide a complete picture of the students' attitudes toward the moral curriculum at Central High School.

Data were collected in the original language, which is Mandarin Chinese, and then translated into English. Although the initial analysis was done in the field, a more substantial analysis was conducted in the United States. Both quantitative and qualitative computer programs were used to help analyze and make sense of the data.

All interview accounts were not recorded due to the concerns of informants even though anonymity was ensured for each informant. The English version of the accounts was analyzed with ATLAS.ti, a qualitative software program with code-retriever and theory builder functions. The ATLAS.ti program takes the grounded theory approach, which is "a systematic, qualitative procedure to generate a theory that explains, at a broad conceptual level, a process, an action, or interaction about a substantial topic" (Creswell 2002: 439).

The ATLAS.ti program claims it can build theory in that propositions can be formulated through a conceptual structure grounded in data. This study does not attempt to develop a theory. Rather, it is built on Bronfenbrenner's (1979) ecological theory of human development. Guided by human ecological theory, this study takes advantage of the ATLAS.ti program's systematic coding to extract themes and findings that are grounded in data. With the ATLAS.ti program, the interview accounts are coded, higher-order classification and categories are developed, and several themes are extracted.

The Statistical Package for Social Sciences [SPSS] software was used to analyze the questionnaire data, which was initially recorded in hand charts. SPSS helped generate descriptive statistics that provided background information about the students and confirmed the findings obtained from the interview analysis. At the same time, the ATLAS.ti program helped clarify, explain and illustrate the statistical findings.

## Validity and Generalizability

Validity has long been a key issue in the debate over the legitimacy of qualitative research. Traditional categories of validity are based on a positivist assumption that underlies quantitative and experimental research.

Many qualitative researchers have begun to reconceptualize validity that is suitable for qualitative inquiry.

Guba and Lincoln (1989) propose the concept of "authenticity"(p. 245) as a substitute for validity in qualitative inquiry, which refers to a balanced presentation of all perspectives, values and beliefs. It involves "fairness" (p. 245) in the reporting of different views and conflicts, "ontological authenticity" (Guba and Lincoln 1989:248) which describes the values and beliefs beneath such discrepancies, and "catalytic authenticity" (p. 248) which refers to the usefulness of the study for other cases.

Maxwell (1992) conceptualizes validity based on the kinds of understanding of the studied phenomenon, rather than on the research procedures that are utilized in the prevailing positivist tradition. He proposes a typology of validity for qualitative studies: descriptive validity, interpretive validity, theoretical validity, generalization, and evaluative validity. Descriptive validity is the factual accuracy of an account; interpretive validity refers to the meanings of the account to the people engaged; and theoretical validity is the account's validity as a theory of some phenomenon, including the theoretical constructs and the theoretical relationship among these constructs. He suggests that these three types of validity are most directly involved in assessing a qualitative account in relation to the actual situation on which the account is based.

Qualitative researchers also try to redefine generalizability to make it suitable for qualitative work (Schofield 1990). Guba and Lincoln (1981, 1982) argue that generalizations are impossible since no phenomenon is time-free or context-free and that the transferability from one situation to another depends on the degree of similarity between the two situations. They propose to use "fittingness" to replace generalizability in qualitative inquiry. The logical development of their argument leads to an approach that places emphasis on providing substantial information about the entity studied and the setting in which that entity is situated (Schofield 1990). Without such information it is impossible to make an informed judgment about whether the conclusions of one study are useful in understanding other sites.

Schofield (1990) argues that one of the approaches for increasing generalizability as perceived by qualitative researchers is to study "what is, " that is, "to study the typical, the common or the ordinary" (p. 209). She suggests that site selection based on typicality is far more likely to increase the potential generalizability of the study than selection on the basis of convenience or ease of access. By choosing a typical case, the researcher "maximizes the fit between the research site and what is more broadly in society" (p. 210).

This study strives to achieve validity and generalizability as conceptualized by qualitative researchers. First, this study attempts to achieve descriptive validity through careful documentation of field notes and interview accounts. Data is triangulated through observation, interview and questionnaire and then compared for any inconsistency. Second, this study attends interpretive validity by soliciting emic viewpoints in the natural setting of a single case in order to understand the meanings that people ascribe to their behaviors. Third, this study tries to achieve theoretical validity, asking colleagues for their feedback and input and confirming terminology of theoretical constructs through academic exchanges within the research community.

In addition, this study strives to achieve authenticity as conceptualized by Guba and Lincoln (1989). It is believed that there is no researcher-independent account. Instead of claiming that the researcher is free from any bias, this study takes advantage of the researcher's unique role as an outsider who previously experienced the moral education curriculum as a student in Chinese secondary schools. It tries to give a complete presentation of the students' attitudes toward the moral education curriculum. It presents not only the mainstream opinions but also the marginal opinions of the students with regard to the moral education curriculum. It further describes any conflicts or contradictions revealed in students' attitudes and the values, ideological beliefs and worldviews underlying their attitudes.

Finally, given the variety and the geographically unbalanced development of secondary school education in China, it is impossible for a single research study to capture the complete picture of Chinese secondary school moral education practice. The current study limits itself to Central High School, a small part of a much larger picture. It seeks to draw a small but authentic portrait of moral education in an urban state-run secondary school in Southwestern China. It is believed that "fittingness," that is, the similarity between the entity studied and the settings to which the conclusion applies, rather than classical generalizability is a better criterion for this case study. Therefore, this study places emphasis on collecting and analyzing substantial information for the case studied and the setting in which this case is situated. It seeks to enable the reader to make an informed judgment about whether the conclusions of this study are useful in understanding other sites.

# 4

# A DESCRIPTION OF CENTRAL HIGH SCHOOL

## Socio-Economic Background

Central high school is situated in a provincial capital city in the southwest of China. The city is the fourth largest city in China in terms of population. It covers 12,390 square kilometers, with 7 districts, 4 satellite cities and 8 counties in its administrative area (Tao and Wang 1999).

The ongoing economic reform spurring the transition from a socialist planned economy to a market economy in the past 20 decades has had a great impact on the development of the city. In the years since the establishment of the People's Republic of China, the city has become industrialized, especially military-related industries. For example, 49 large-scale military-related enterprises moved to the city from other parts of China during the 10 years spanning China's seventh and eighth five-year national development plans. In the past decades many of these state-sponsored and subsidized enterprises have been losing money due to the downsizing of the military force and the increasing competition brought about by the market driven economy (Tao and Wang 1999).

The state-sector reform in the city, which started in 1993, intensified after 1996. One hundred and nine (109) out of 415 state enterprises have gone bankrupted or merged under the policy of state-enterprise reform. In 1998, there were 95 state-enterprises that went bankrupt, merged or became privatized in the city; about 100,000 state-enterprise employees were laid-off, compared with 52,000 in 1997. In recent years, the economic growth rate in the city remained low while the unemployment rate continued to rise. There was a growing polarization among people of different economic statuses with the laid off workers at the bottom level (Tao and Wang 1999).

Central High School is located in one of the seven districts in the center of the city. Many of its students come from the industrial area of the city where a majority of the parents work or used to work for the state-enterprises. According to the student questionnaire, 60 percent of the fathers and 64 percent of the mothers belonged to the working class while only 18 percent of the fathers and 11 percent of the mothers were professionals (see Table B-2, Appendix B). Moreover, 11 percent of the fathers were reported being laid-off from their state jobs with another 9 percent expecting to be laid-off soon. Also, 15 percent of the mothers were reported being laid-off and another 10 percent expecting to be laid-off soon (see Table B-3, Appendix B). It is clear that many the students' families are suffering financial hardship from the economic policy changes. Forty six percent (46 percent) of the students' families have monthly household incomes below 1,000 Chinese yuan, equivalent to about 125 U.S. dollars (see Table B-4, Appendix B).

## Historical Development

According to official statistics, there were 558 secondary schools enrolling 361,200 students under the administration of the city in 1998 (Tao and Wang 1999). Only 39 secondary schools are located in the seven districts in the metropolitan area, while the rest are spread out among the surrounding cities, counties and villages.

There were 1,325 students enrolled at Central High School in the 1998–1999 school year, including 408 students in the senior level and 917 students in the junior level. Under the 9-year compulsory education system in China, all graduates from elementary schools are promoted to junior high school without an entrance examination. However, the entrance to senior secondary schools is highly competitive, with about half of the students entering the regular senior high school while the other half enrolling at professional or technical high schools. As a result, there were many more junior high students than senior high students at Central High School.

Central High School is located in a neighborhood that is heavily populated. The school is surrounded by small narrow streets over 100 years old that survived the Japanese bombing in World War II. There are many small shops on both sides of the street including book rental businesses, gift shops, printing and copying shops and restaurants. It is common for students to gather in the small, crowded restaurants during lunchtime. There are also peddlers near the school entrance, trying to sell snacks and other items to the students. These small businesses often make the street outside the school gate dirty and untidy. Sometimes a school official will show up and try to drive them away, especially when the school is expecting visitors and inspection.

Central High School is not isolated from its surroundings. Rather, it is open to the world outside. Unlike the majority of schools in the cities, Central High School does not have a wall to separate it from its neighborhood. In the past some residents next to the school expanded their houses by adding an additional room abutting the original school wall. Most of the original wall was torn down during construction of the new school building; however, one section of the original wall still stands with the neighbors' homes adjacent to it. For a long time after the construction was completed, the school did not have a gate because the school and its neighbors disputed the boundary line between them. The absence of a wall separating the school from the outside world is a useful image symbolizing the intruding forces of society, which will be elaborated on in later chapters.

Central High School has a small campus of 11,234 square meters. A recently built four-floor school building, together with two other small buildings, occupies almost half of the campus. The basketball court is in the middle of the small, unpaved playground. There are a few trees, but no grass lawns on the campus. Hundreds of bicycles, the main transportation means of the teachers and students, are parked in the basement of the new building.

At the entrance of the school, a quotation from one of Deng Xiaoping's speeches is written on the wall. A slogan is painted on the back wall of the neighboring houses. There are two bulletin boards near the entrance, where announcements and daily attendance are posted.

Central High School was formerly a primary school for girls founded in 1895 by the Canadian Methodist Mission. In 1915 a middle school was added. The school became a private high school for girls in 1938. The school's named was changed to Central High School in 1952. It continued to be a girls' school until 1968 when China abolished all single-sex schools. Now Central High School is a state-run high school with 1,325 students, ranging from the seventh to the twelfth grades, with 132 teachers and 31 administrative workers.

Central High School consists of two levels: the junior level and the senior level. The junior high level enrolls students who have graduated from local elementary schools. In general, very few elementary students fail the graduation exam and have to repeat the 6th grade before they are promoted to junior high school. However, the examination to enter senior high is much more competitive. Each year about 50 percent of the junior high graduates at Central High School are promoted to its senior high school while the other 50 percent of the students are either absorbed by various vocational schools or enter the labor market.

Generally, the students at Central High School are ranked about average or below average when their grades are compared to the same-age students in the metropolitan area. In addition to the students promoted from within the junior level, Central High School also admits a small number of qualified students from outside the community, including students whose entrance examination scores do not meet the requirements for more prestigious schools and those whose schools have no senior high level.

In 1994, the school's slogan was "Work Hard to Regain the Past Glory." Before it was taken over by the Communist government, the school was a prestigious private school. It had a beautiful campus combining Western and Chinese architectural styles. It had a two-story music building and a swimming pool. The school's curriculum emphasized English and music. It focused on students' character and behavior as well as domestic skills and health. It received high marks from the Nationalist government regarding students' academic performance and conduct. In the early years of the People's Republic, Central High School still enjoyed a high academic standing. It produced many highly accomplished graduates including a Ph.D. degree holder from Cornell University, a senior conductor of the China Central Opera Company and winner of many international prizes, and a general and president of the General Hospital of the People's Liberation Army.

After being taken over by the Communist government, especially after the establishment of the key-school policy, Central High School lost its prestige status. The local educational committee began to establish key schools in 1963. The purpose was to make the best use of limited resources in order to produce skilled labor. Five high schools were chosen in 1963 and 25 high schools were chosen in 1978 based on their reputation, academic excellence, strong teaching staff, facilities and many other factors. These key schools were given priority in the allocation of the most talented teachers, students and facilities. Central High School was not chosen as a key school largely due to its small campus, although it had the highest rate of graduates entering universities and colleges among all schools in the city in 1961–1962. Since then Central High School has become a school with less talented students and teachers and insufficient facilities. The original buildings were torn down in order to accommodate an increasing number of students.

Another big challenge the school experienced came with the launch of the market economy reforms. The market economy and competition have greatly impacted education. As part of the process of educational system decentralization, the local educational committee began in 1984 to experiment in some key schools with the principal-responsibility system and the teacher-employment system. Under the new systems, the principal becomes the legal representative of the school and is responsible for academics, administration and finance. The principal has the power to hire teachers and establish teachers' salaries and bonuses based on their performance, unlike prior years when the local educational committee assigned all teachers to their jobs and all salaries adhered to the same standard. The new systems have significantly motivated teachers and teachers' incomes have finally become more in line with their duties compared with other occupations. Some schools are even able to build new apartment buildings to house their teachers.

Central High School adopted the new systems in 1996. Because of its non-key school status and poor resources, Central High School has difficulty in finding the resources to give the teachers bonuses, which have become a large portion of a person's income under the new market economy. Unlike key schools or other more academically competitive schools, Central High School does not receive much funding from the government. More importantly, while many parents are willing to pay a large fee to assure a place for their children in key schools, the parents of Central High School students do not have such income resources. Compared with teachers who work at key schools, teachers at Central High School are paid much less and many of them have housing problems.

In order to survive in the highly competitive school market, the current leadership of Central High School has been striving for the status of key school. Believing achievement leads to status, the school is motivated to catch up with key schools. The principal makes it clear in her speeches that it is a major goal of Central High School to become a key school in the future. She believes Central High School has the potential to be chosen to be a key school and encourages the teachers to work extra hard to improve the students' academic performance and promote Central High School in a variety of ways. According to the principal, only impressive academic achievement will prompt the Educational Committee to give the school more financial support, benefiting both teachers and students.

Central High School has been trying to build its future on its past legacy. It draws strength from its history as an all-female school. In the fall of 1997, Central High School established its first all-girl class in the seventh grade. Two more seventh grade all-girl classes were established the next year. The all-girl classes focus on the teaching of the English language and creativity.

Central High School is the only school in the city that has all-girl classes. However, according to a school official, Central High School will not experiment with an all-girl class in its senior level, fearing that female students cannot compete with male students on the college entrance exam and thereby negatively affect the school's academic record. The all-girl class experiment is important for the school largely because it is believed that it will benefit the school's image and status.

Another strategy of the school leadership is to promote creativity education. *The Guideline for Educational Reform and Development in China* (CCPCC and State Council 1993) called for a transition from exam-oriented education to quality-oriented education. Creativity is a hot issue although it is quite new for Chinese schools. In 1993 Central High School put up a sign referring to itself as the Creativity School of Science and Technology. Only the junior level has creativity classes while the senior sector is still focusing on preparing students for the college entrance exam. There are 19 classes and 917 students in the junior level, but only one teacher, a chemistry teacher by training, teaches creativity. Although the teaching of creativity is a very small part of the school teaching, Central High School is the only school in the city that bears the title of Creativity School. Four of its students have obtained patents for their inventions.

The school is involved in various educational research activities. All teachers at Central High School are required to participate in the by-weekly meetings of its various educational research groups. Every teacher is required to submit one research paper each year. Central High School's active involvement in educational research activities has increased its popularity. In recent years, Central High School has received many visitors, including 300 teachers and administrators from 150 different institutions all over the country. In the fall of 1998, it became the only non-key school that was chosen as a visiting site during a national conference on quality education.

Another example that reflects the Central High School's effort and commitment to elevate its academic standing is its incentive policy. For those students who make significant contributions to Central High School or win fame for the school, the school will honor them by permanently displaying their photos. For those who achieve national recognition, the school will regard them as heroes of the school and place their names in the historic records of the school.

Central High School also makes great efforts to improve students' test scores. The daily school schedule for students can extend up to 12 hours. Both teachers and students, especially those of graduating classes, are required to attend classes after normal school hours on weekdays and also a half day or whole day of classes on Saturdays during the semester. They are also asked to attend classes for several weeks during the summer vacation and for at least one week during the winter vacation.

Another strategy used to improve students' scores is to increase competition among the students. In each grade of the senior level, students are grouped into advanced classes, average classes and slow classes according to their test scores. The students take several exams during the school year and these scores determine whether they go up or down or maintain their status. The students with the highest scores are grouped into advanced classes, which are taught by the most competent teachers and have the most strict class management. A student in an advanced class has a better chance of entering a college or university.

As a result of such practices, Central High School has improved its students' test scores. Both the rate of its high school graduates going to college and the percentage of junior students graduating to the senior level have gone up despite the students' poor academic background. Both its senior and junior levels have received awards from the Educational Committee in 1991–1998. In fact, in 1998 Central High School became the top non-key school in the city in terms of the rate of graduates entering colleges and universities.

Through all these efforts, Central High School has improved its credentials remarkably. Its all-girl classes and its creativity experiment have attracted a great deal of attention. The improvements in students' test scores as well as the research achievements of teachers have gained increased recognition for the school. The school's leadership continues to carry out their educational mission with a strong determination and commitment to achieve key school status. However, the competition is severe. Central High School is moving closer, but has not yet reached its goal to become a key school.

## Administrative Structure

The administrative system of moral education in all Chinese elementary and secondary schools is a unified system (Hu 1998). At Central High School, with the principal-responsibility system, the secretary of the CCP branch only plays an auxiliary role in moral education. A vice principal is designated to be in charge of moral education and leads a moral education team made up of *zhengjiaochu* (the Political and Ideological Education Department), *gongqingtuang* (the Communist Youth League), *shaoxiandui* (the Young Pioneers production brigade), *xueshenghui* (Student Association) and *banzhuren* (class masters).

## Political and Ideological Education Department

The Politics and Ideology Department at Central High School is staffed with two directors and four teachers. Each teacher heads one division: the Communist Youth League, the Young Pioneer production brigade, the Student Association, and the division of problem behavior and security. This department is responsible for ideological and political work, student behavior and conduct, student physical well-being, sports and amusement activities, campus environment and school security. Its tasks are wide-ranging including flag ceremonies; school-wide activities such as field trips, sports meets, singing contests; recruitment for the Communist Youth League and the Young Pioneer production brigade; evaluation of the class master, class collectives and students, and so on.

The focus of the Political and Ideology Department, however, as a director of the department pointed out, is on *changgui jiaoyu* (everyday behavior cultivation). Everyday, the staff members in the department take attendance for teachers and students, deal with problem students referred to them, supervise eye exercise and physical exercise, inspect the cleanness of classrooms as the students complete their cleaning chores and put these results on the school bulletin board. According to another director of the department, as trivial and boring as these tasks may be, they are at least tangible. She suggested that their jobs are much more substantive than the empty talks on ideology in the past.

According to the same director, it is difficult to get teachers to work in the department and the staff members usually stay for a year or two and then leave the department. The staff members are considered half time, with the exception of the two directors, and they all teach at least one subject to fulfill the other half time. Since they teach a subject half time the staff also belong to *jiaowuchu* (the Department of Instruction). But they are paid less than the full-time subject teachers in that department. The staff members complained that the school regards their positions in the Political and Ideological Department as less important. A staff member in charge of problem behavior and campus safety said, "You have to have the spirit of a candle to work here—to sacrifice yourself."

There are no specific qualifications or training required for the positions in the Political and Ideological Department. One of the staff members, a voice teacher who transferred from a teacher training school in a remote area, felt at a loss when she suddenly became the counselor of the Young Pioneers production brigade at the Central High School six years ago. She did not know what she was supposed to do. Nobody gave her any training or instruction. She had to learn by herself as she went along. Only recently did she learn the appropriate procedure for conducting a flag-raising ceremony.

It has become increasingly difficult for the Political and Ideology Department to organize other activities besides daily behavior education. One of the vice principals suggested field trips are scarce because nowadays it is hard to find transportation and places willing to receive the students without money. In addition, the school schedule is filled with overtime classes, and there is hardly any time for extra-curricular activities. A staff member in charge of the Student Association and the Student Broadcasting Station explained that the academic classes use up all the school hours and it is almost impossible for him to organize moral education activities. The school basketball competition he organized had to be held during the lunch break. He said, "Sweeping streets is what we do most often."

There is a nationwide tendency for Chinese schools to be inconsistent in and neglect the teaching of moral education (CCPCC 1994). It is not surprising that at Central High School, moral education is not valued as highly as the teaching of academics. The dominance of academics in the school leaves little room for conducting moral education. The department staff view their tasks are unpleasant as well as burdensome. Plus, they are paid less than teachers of other subjects.

## Class Masters

A class or *ban* is the basic functional unit in which moral education is taught. The class master is an important channel to cultivate the desired ideology and character among the students and instruct them in their overall development (SEC 1998b). Class masters are teachers who are each assigned to one ban of approximately 50 students and charged with their moral well being. The *ban* is assigned an identifying number and a permanent classroom to which subject teachers come to teach. The class master usually teaches one subject to the *ban* and stays with the *ban* throughout the junior high and senior high school years. The function of the class master is a combination of homeroom teacher and guidance counselor (Chan 1997).

At Central High School, there are 27 class masters with 8 in the senior secondary level and 19 in the junior secondary level. Class masters are considered crucial in conducting moral education because they interact face-to-face with the students on a daily basis, spend a great amount of time with the students, and are involved in every aspect of student life. The class masters were expected to advise the students in many areas: ideology, morality, conduct, academics, health, personal hygiene, and after class activities. As Chan (1997) suggested, the scope of subjects that class masters are supposed to cover in guiding their students is very wide. They are expected to advise students on all areas of life, and to prevent the students from exposure to harmful materials and involvements.

The class masters at Central High School are supposed to supervise the students all the time unless a subject teacher is with them. The class masters are required to provide six presence, which means they must not only attend class master meetings and staff political studies but also conduct class meetings and supervise the students during the flag-raising ceremonies, physical exercise and eye exercise and students' self-study periods. Compared with subject teachers, the class masters have much more work to do and spend longer hours at school. The head masters are not paid very much for their extra work. Usually they receive a small amount of money monthly for class master duties. The position may be unattractive to many teachers. However, the experience of being a class master is considered very important for a teacher, especially when promotions are being considered. A teacher's professional status largely depends upon his or her experience as a class master (Chan 1997). Therefore, although the teachers may be reluctant, they all have to be class masters some time during their teaching career.

Class masters have much more power and control over the students in their class compared to subject teachers. They are supposed to discipline the students or even contact their parents for their behavior problems, which most students dread. The class masters also prepare written evaluations of the students, which will be placed in their permanent personal profile. Because the subject teachers only interact with the students during class periods and have little control over the students after class, the students usually behave much better in their class master's class than in a subject teacher's class. It would be normal for a noisy classroom to suddenly become quiet when a class master shows up outside the window during a subject teacher's period.

At Central High School, especially in its senior section, class masters are usually those who teach major academic subjects, such as Chinese, math, English, physics, and chemistry. It is very rare for a Physical Education teacher or a Politics teacher to be assigned as class master. Students tend to study the class master's subject more seriously than other subjects. Also the class master has more control over time that can be used for extra studying. For example, the class master is supposed to conduct class meetings every week. Sometimes, however, the class master uses this time to teach his/her subject.

The appointment of class masters at Central High School reflects the school's favoritism for the high-achieving classes. Typically the class masters in the advanced classes tend to be the most experienced, capable and responsible teachers in the school. They are usually good at teaching their subjects and managing the individual students as well as the *ban* collective.

Although the duty of the class master is primarily to further patriotic, collectivist, socialist education (SEC 1998b), class masters at Central High School tend to focus their attention on making each class a good environment for improving student's academic performance. One class master named Li Zhao (1998) (pseudonym) summarized this aim in her work report dated in 1998. The first task she accomplished was organizing the students to study school regulations and rules, such as *Quantitative Measurement of Student Conduct, Regulations for Managing Student Behavior, Ten Rules of Central High School, Student Classroom Rules, Goals for Constructing Class Collective,* and *Class Rules.* These rules are primarily intended to advance students' academic performance.

Her second accomplishment was holding two parents' meetings in which the students were included. At the meetings, the principal discusses the school's policy and strategies to prepare students for the national college entrance exam and the graduation exam. These meetings create the desired pressure and competition among students so that they are more motivated to improve their academic performance.

The last accomplishment in her list was improving students' overall development. She encouraged students to participate in various activities, such as speech contests, debates, themed class meetings, a New Year party, small plays, sports meets, wall-newspapers and donations to flood relief (Zhao 1998).

Central High School's leadership pays great attention to the performance of the class masters. The class masters are evaluated according to the performance of their class as well as their own performance. For example, they score points when the class in their charge is given any awards and they lose points for behavior problems occurring in the class. As a vice principle explained, the class masters are the soul of their class. Their role as the soul, however, is largely one that facilitates the learning environment of their class and advances the academic performance of the students through a large variety of activities.

## Subject Teachers

According to the Guideline for Moral Education at Secondary Schools (SEC 1995), subject teachers and all other staff at each school should integrate moral education in their teaching. All teachers have the professional duty to *jiaoshu yuren* (teach the book and nurture the person). However, the subject teachers at Central High School have limited contact with their students. For each class, their time with the students is usually limited to one 50-minute period each day. The subject teachers are under pressure to raise the students' test scores in their subjects. They push the students to work hard in their subjects. For example, the noon-break is highly sought by the subject teachers. As a result, the focus of the subject teachers is on teaching their subjects rather than nurturing character.

## Researcher as Participant Observer

Before being accepted by Central High School, my research proposal was turned down by a key school. This school was a well-known key school that is located in one of the city's most prosperous commercial areas. Recently, this school's building was converted into a fashionable modern office building with the help of developers who now share part of the building with the school. The key school possesses skilled teachers and students with good academic performance. Many parents are willing to pay a large sum of money to enroll their children in this school. The principal apparently was not particularly interested in having me doing research.

Afterwards, I approached Central High School through a personal connection. My research proposal was accepted by the leadership of the school largely because they are interested in educational experimentation and research projects, which they consider an important strategy to promote the status of the school.

Since my research is in the area of moral education at the senior secondary school level, the school leadership arranged for me to closely observe the class master of an advanced eleventh grade class and how she conducted moral education in her class. I was allowed to do classroom observation and conduct interviews with students and teachers in this class. I volunteered to be a full-time English teacher, but my request was declined. Instead, the only teaching assignment given to me was to teach conversational English as an extra-curricular activity to the experimental all-girl classes in the junior level.

These arrangements were not in writing. In fact the issue of a written contract was never mentioned by the school officials. As my research progressed, my involvement in the school grew. I was asked to give seminars on study strategies, research methods, American culture and the U.S. school system, and so forth. The scope of my observation and interviews extended across the entire school. However, I made sure that all of my duties had no potential of interfering with the learning activities of the students, especially those considered promising candidates to do well on the national college entrance examination.

In the class to which I was originally assigned, I observed the teachers and students in their routine activities, including classes and doing exercises. I attended their sports meets, singing contests, New Year party and other activities. I also attended teacher-parent meetings and met some of the parents. Later in the fall semester, I was asked to help with a school play in English in a district competition. When the head teacher was in the hospital, I was asked to help supervise the students in her class. I took the opportunity to hold a class discussion on cheating on exams and assigned the journal topic "What Is a Moral Person?" to the students.

In the other slow class, I had many long and in-depth conversations with the students because these students had less study pressure and more free time. Actually, because they had so much free time, the class master asked me to teach them conversational English in their two periods of self-study each week. For the class master, he found someone to supervise the students; for the students they could learn something practical; for me it was a good opportunity to interact with the students.

Since I was teaching conversational English, a course that did not require grades or exams, I chose topics that were most helpful in revealing the students' values and ideology. I talked with them about their life ideals and what they would do with their money if they became millionaires. Often, our conversation would last long after the class period was over.

Most of these students were interested in my life in America. They also told me their personal issues, for example, who they were dating and problems with their parents and teachers. Some of the students became my friends. They were warm and eager to talk to me when they saw me at school. They wanted to meet me outside school. There were two girls in particular who arranged to meet me on Saturdays to practice their English. They became good informants for my understanding of their fellow students.

Besides casual conversations and class discussions, I was able to conduct structured in-depth interviews with students randomly selected from three different classes in three different grades. I first interviewed the students in my office at the school and found they were very reserved once they came to the office. I found out later it was because the office I was using in the political-ideological education department was usually considered the place for punishing problem students.

I later conducted interviews with the students over lunch at small restaurants near the school. The lunch break was the only time in their busy schedules that the students were available for a one-hour interview. Some students could not go home for lunch due to the distance. So it worked out well. I also found that when I treated the students to lunch, they tended to see it as a friendly gesture and opened up to me easily. In conclusion, Central High School was a rather open and supportive research site for this study.

# 5

## STUDENT ATTITUDES TOWARD THE MORAL EDUCATION CURRICULUM

The findings of this study will be presented in this chapter. In accordance with Cuban's (1992) curriculum typology, this chapter will analyze students' attitudes toward the moral education curriculum at Central High School.

### Curriculum Typology

According to Jackson (1992), the definition of curriculum should be expanded to include not only the planned activities and materials but also the unplanned experiences that occur in school. These unplanned experiences include not only all the incidental learning of a positive nature but also those experiences that lead to undesirable, even harmful outcomes. Jackson suggests that there are two separate sets of curricula: the explicitly endorsed curriculum and the unintended or hidden curriculum (1968).

Some of the negative outcomes are believed to be the product of institutional qualities, over which teachers may have little control. There is an increasing scholarly interest in the possibility that schools do harm and do it systematically to many students (Jackson 1992).

Cuban (1992) takes a political perspective to approach the issue of curriculum change and stability. According to Cuban, there are many forces at multiple levels that shape the making of curriculum. The principals and teachers reshape the curriculum as it is implemented in their schools.

Therefore, the adoption and implementation of the curriculum can be considered primarily a political rather than a technical process.

Cuban (1992) divides curriculum into three types: intended curriculum, taught curriculum and learned curriculum (see Fig. 1). Labeled as "recommended," "adopted," "official," "formal," or "explicit" (p. 222) the intended curriculum is that body of content contained in state frameworks, district courses of study, listing of courses taught in a program, and syllabi. It is the subject matter, skills, and values that policymakers expect to be taught.

The taught curriculum is sometimes called the "implicit," "delivered," or "operational" (Cuban 1992:222) curriculum. It is what the teachers do and use to present content, ideas, skills, and attitudes. It is through the taught curriculum that the intended curriculum is altered by teachers' beliefs and the school's agenda. Cuban also suggests that in the taught curriculum there are formal and informal lessons.

At the school level, for example, the hidden curriculum is taught as the school chooses its own focus on the courses, staffing, and the use of space. At the classroom level, the hidden curriculum is taught through teachers' behavior, for instance, the ways teachers handle cheating on tests or letting a student sleep in class.

The learned curriculum is what the students have learned as a result of being in a classroom (Cuban 1992). Often, the gap between what is taught and what is learned—both intended and unintended, is large. For instance, when students covertly negotiate with their teachers over rules and requirements in the classroom, these negotiations can serve as a kind of learning experience about the nature of schooling, work, and their power.

While the moral curriculum that the Chinese government intends to teach the youngsters in school is considered the intended moral curriculum, the moral education curriculum that is actually taught at Central High School can be viewed as the taught moral curriculum. This study examines students' attitudes toward not only the content of the officially intended moral curriculum but also the adoption and implementation of the intended moral curriculum by teachers and administrators at Central High School.

It finds students at Central High School have rather negative attitudes toward the official content of the intended moral curriculum such as collectivism, patriotism, socialism and the leadership of the CCP. It also finds that students have negative attitudes toward the taught moral curriculum as well.

## The Intended Moral Curriculum

As the body of moral content contained in government directives and textbooks, course guidelines and syllabi, the intended moral curriculum is the values and ideology that the government wants to instill among the students (Cuban 1992). The content of the intended moral curriculum in Chinese schools is all encompassing and complex. Unlike in the West where morality has little to do with ideology or politics, morality in China is intertwined with ideology and politics. Morality is defined in terms of correct ideology and politics. Moral education in China consists of ideology, political thought, moral behavior, psychological traits, and concepts pertinent to modern society such as the market and commodity, of which the latter two have been added in recent years.

Not all the components receive the same amount of attention; some are emphasized more than others. In fact, psychological traits and concepts pertinent to modern society are largely ignored in moral education practice at Central High School. Therefore, this study does not cover every component of the all-inclusive content of the moral education curriculum. Rather, it focuses on students' attitudes towards the topics that are most frequently taught at Central High School, including collectivism, patriotism, the CCP, socialism and Marxist philosophy.

## Collectivism

Collectivism is the core of socialist morality. The essence of collectivism is to sacrifice one's own good for the good of the collective. This study finds that the majority of students at Central High School have negative attitudes towards collectivism. Over half of the respondents (51 percent) do not believe the majority of students would put the welfare of the collective above their own. Almost one third of the students (29 percent) do not give their opinions. Only 20 percent of the respondents believe the majority of students would put the welfare of the collective above their own (see Table B-5, Appendix B). In addition, about half of the respondents (49 percent) do not believe that the purpose of human life is to sacrifice for others. Over one third of the respondents (34 percent) give a neutral response to the question. A small number of the respondents (17 percent) believe that the purpose of human life is to sacrifice for others (see Table B-6, Appendix B).

It is not surprising that the majority of the students at Central High School do not believe in collectivism. Previous studies have revealed that

Chinese youth are becoming more resistant to collective values and that individualism among them was especially strong in the 1990s (Rosen 1989, 1994). The current study confirms that the majority of Chinese secondary school students have embraced individualism.

It is noteworthy that as many as one-third of the respondents choose neutral positions in responding to the questions. In fact, although the return rate of the questionnaire is very high (95 percent), as many as one-third of the respondents choose neutral responses to questions regarding values and ideologies. According to a long article on the first page of the *Beijing Youth Daily* written collectively by the paper's youth section, the "new mantra" of university students is said to be "it doesn't matter" (Youth Section, *Beijing Youth Daily*, August 19, 1993:1, cited in Rosen 1994:2). Rosen observed that the current malaise among college students is so severe that it seems necessary to include "it doesn't matter" on questionnaires to ensure more accurate answers.

Students in the 1980s tended to give rather conformist answers according to what they thought the teacher would consider a correct answer (Rosen 1989). Yet students in the 1990s seem indifferent. They did not care to wrestle with moral-ideological issues. As one interviewee says, "Our attitudes toward moral teachings have changed from aversion to indifference. We have grown up. We have listened to the same thing for over ten years. We are no longer interested in it." Therefore, it is fair to say that the large number of students giving neutral answers reflects their indifference toward collectivism. Furthermore, such indifference among students suggests that "skepticism and malaise" among university students (Rosen 1994:2) has spread to secondary students.

In the in-depth interviews, interviewees were given a real case of a female student who has to choose between her own interest and the interest of the school. She is a student leader and will graduate from the junior sector next year. She has the potential to enter a key school but her current school does not want to lose her because of her leadership skills and the good example she provides for her fellow students.

Nineteen (19) of the 21 interviewees believe that she should leave and enroll at the key school in order to secure a better future. As one student states, " I would definitely choose to go to a better school. Most students put individual benefit over collective benefit. Nobody would believe the meaning of life is sacrifice. To reach one's personal goal is more important."

Another student remarks, "In her situation everybody would choose to leave the school. It is important to pursue one's own potential." Another student says, "One's own future depends on oneself. Of course one's own good is above the collective good."

These students exhibit a cynical attitude toward collectivism. One student points out that collectivism is unrealistic in a market economy. "Nowadays people move from one collective to another. It is impossible to love all the collectives that one is associated with."

Only one student believes that the majority of students would put collective benefit above individual benefit. She states that everyone in her class worked hard as a group in the singing contest in order to win the award for the class collective. But at the same time she points out that the motive of many students was to gain points for their conduct evaluation.

In conclusion, both interview data and questionnaire data suggest that students at Central High School have rather negative attitudes toward collectivism. A majority of them despise self-sacrifice and put their own interest above the interest of the collective. This finding supports the observation of a Chinese researcher mentioned in Rosen's study that the values of Chinese youth today bear a striking resemblance to the Western humanistic philosophy of self-actualization (Rosen 1994).

## Patriotism, Socialism, and the CCP

Patriotism has been the most important theme of the moral education curriculum, especially after the Guideline of Patriotic Education was issued in 1995. Patriotism in China is closely related to politics. With the decline of Marxist ideology, China's leaders seem to be relying on patriotism and nationalism as the key components of a new ideology whose primary purpose is very simple: economic modernization and support of the leadership of the CCP (Ogden 2002). Tu argues that the Chinese government tries to maintain the status quo by holding on to the banner of patriotism (1994).

As Jiang Zemin, the former Chairman of the CCP suggested, to be patriotic is to love socialism and the CCP. The textbook of the Chinese Language and Literature course has adopted his speech entitled "Carry on and Promote Patriotic Tradition in New Historical Period" (Jiang 1990). However, the current study reveals that the majority of students at Central High School are skeptical about so-called patriotism.

According to the student questionnaire, almost half of the respondents (47 percent) are in favor of a separation of patriotism from the love of socialism and the CCP. Only 22 percent of the respondents agree with the association of patriotism with the love of socialism and the CCP. As many as 32 percent of the respondents demonstrate a neutral position on this issue (see Table B-7, Appendix B). As discussed earlier, it is reasonable to believe that those with a neutral position are indifferent to the association between patriotism and political orientation.

The in-depth interviews confirm these responses. Sixteen (16) of the 21 interviewees disagree with the notion that patriotism has to be associated with the love of socialism and the CCP. To these students, patriotism is affection for one country independent from one political orientation, and therefore it is possible for one to love one country without conforming to any kind of political system or ideology. As one student suggests,

> Patriotism does not equal love for the CCP and socialism. I learned from history class that political parties are all hypocritical. The CCP always says good things about itself. It was the same with the Nationalist Party. I don't want to join any parties. I can love the country without associating myself with any parties. I did not want to join the Communist Youth League either. But I was pushed in. I think patriotism should be mani-fested through specific actions. It is hypocritical to just love the political party. My father is a CCP member but he gambles and worships idols. I would love the country, but I don't love the CCP because I only love things that I choose to love myself.

It is obvious that this student does not favor the CCP and its socialist ideology. She questions the credibility of the CCP and the conduct of some of its members. Her father is a CCP member but he is engaged in activities he is not supposed to be engaged in. Gambling is illegal in China and worshipping idols contradicts communist belief. Therefore, she refused to identify patriotism with love of the CCP and socialism.

Another student observes, "I don't think one has to love the CCP and socialism to be called patriotic because patriotic affection can be manifested in many ways." One student supports his argument with the example of the patriotic overseas Chinese. "Many overseas Chinese have made contribu-tions to China's development through donation and other activities. They don't necessarily agree with the CCP and the socialist system. But one cannot say they are not patriotic."

Only 5 of the 21 interviewees believe that patriotism is inseparable from political orientation. To these students, since the CCP is the only ruling party, it has made its socialist ideology into the only acceptable ideology, which permeates every aspect of social life in China. As one student suggests, "To love the country one must love the CCP and the socialist ideology, for everything is considered as an expression of the love of the CCP and its ideology." Another student says, "In China, one has to love the CCP and socialism to be considered patriotic. The country is under the rule of the CCP. How can one love the country without loving its ideology?"

To these students, the CCP dominates all aspects of Chinese life, and thus it is impossible to separate patriotism from political orientation. However, such an attitude does not necessarily suggest these students are in favor of the CCP and socialism. In fact, only 1 of these students states that the leadership of the CCP is correct and the Chinese people should follow its leadership. But he does not explain why.

In addition, this study finds that the majority of students at Central High School do not support the socialist system in China and they seem frustrated with the so-called socialism with Chinese Characteristics. Established by Deng Xiaoping as the theoretical guideline for the reform program, socialism with Chinese Characteristics is a theoretical mixture of socialist political system and market economy (White 1995). Within this guideline, China will maintain its socialist political system while transforming its socialist planned economic system into a market economy.

Although official rhetoric supports the theory of socialism with Chinese Characteristics, to most students, the country has become more capitalist than socialist. As one student points out, "Nowadays, the CCP is downplaying ideology. The difference between capitalism and socialism is not big." Another student states, "I don't believe the workers are owners of the factory any more... The workers are kicked out when they are not needed. This is definitely not socialism."

It is clear that many students are frustrated with the paradox of the theory of socialism with Chinese characteristics. As a teacher of a political course points out, the discussion of political economy in the textbook has always been a means to explain and support China's economic policy. According to this teacher, nowadays the economic changes happen so rapidly that the newly revised textbook cannot provide new theories to keep up with the changes. As one student says,

> Our Politics textbook is full of contradictions. I don't like it at all. The politics and political economics parts are especially bad. There are so many things I cannot comprehend. It gives me a headache when I read the textbook and reflect on the social reality. For example, the textbook says capitalism takes advantage of labor but the state-sector doesn't. I don't understand.

Still, some of the students seem indifferent to the socialist ideology sponsored by the CCP. One student explains, "My parent's generation supports socialism and the CCP, but our generation doesn't really care... My major concerns are the national college exam a job. These two things really matter to me and my parents."

In general, the students believe socialist ideology is meaningless to their personal life. Their concerns are centered on the college entrance exam, finding a good job and enjoying life. They are primarily interested in how to survive in China's increasingly competitive market economy. They do not care whether the current system is capitalist or socialist.

In conclusion, the current study finds that the majority of students at Central High School respond negatively towards the CCP and socialism and their association with patriotism. This finding echoes the finding of a study investigating Shanghai senior secondary students' ideological condition in 1997. Ideological confusion existed among Shanghai senior secondary students and one-third of the students disagreed with the official claim that only the CCP and socialism can lead China to wealth and power (C. Li, et al. 1997). This finding also corresponds with Rosen's observation based on his analysis of Chinese survey studies. In post-Mao China political commitment and unquestioning loyalty toward the CCP have declined as students become more independent minded (Rosen 1989).

## Communist Ideal

The study reveals that the majority of students at Central High School have negative responses toward communism in the intended moral curriculum. According to the students' responses to the questionnaire, there is a wide range of students' attitudes toward communism (see Table B-8, Appendix B). First of all, as many as 40 percent of the students choose a neutral position when asked if they believe communism will eventually come true in China. Considering the popular skepticism and malaise among Chinese students (Rosen 1994), this response is not surprising. As discussed earlier, a neutral position could very likely be a response of indifference. It is believed that the majority of students are not interested in the issue of communism.

The in-depth interviews provide evidence of the students' indifference to communism. Firstly, 5 out of 21 interviewees state they are not sure if communism will eventually come true in China. Moreover, their narratives show that they are not interested in this issue either. They do not care about ideological issues. One student explains that communism is nonsense to him, saying, "Why do we have to realize communism? I'm only concerned about the present... I am content with a hundred bucks spending money each month. Why do we have to figure out an ideology?" Apparently he is unconcerned about ideological issues. The Communism ideal is irrelevant to his life.

Another student makes it clear that there is no room for ideological issues such as communism in his life.

> I don't know if communism will come true. I don't think of such things. It may or may not. It has little influence in my personal life. It will largely impact the country. My father wants me to join the CCP. I don't know why...My parents want me to join the CCP. It is supposed to be beneficial to me... Right now the meaning of life for me is to going to college... I have not thought about the meaning of life in the future...there are many issues I haven't thought about. I am under great pressure to study. I cannot afford to split my attention.

Obviously, this student is preoccupied with preparing for the national college entrance exam, which will decide his future. There is no room for the communist ideal in his life. The communist ideal may have an impact on the future of the country, but it has nothing to do with passing his exam or finding a job. He does not know if communism will come true. Neither does he care. He is too busy with day-to-day tasks and responsibilities to figure it out. Such indifference to ideology is a reflection of the characteristics of youth in the 1990s, the so-called "a generation of pragmatism" (Su 1998; Tian 1997).

Secondly, about one third (29 percent) of the questionnaire respondents relate that they do not believe communism will be realized in China. The in-depth interviews yield a similar finding. Eight (8) out of the 21 interviewees strongly believe that communism will never come true. Five (5) of them believe that China's current social and economic situation makes the realization of communism impossible. As one student suggests,

> I think communism will never come true. Based on what I learned about the evolution of human society, China skipped the capitalist stage and lacks a solid economic foundation and wealth. Chinese socialism is still at its beginning stages. Communism is too far away. Besides, the poor character of the people makes it impossible to realize communism.

This student considers wealth and economic stability essential for realizing communism. In his opinion, China does not have the capacity to become a communist society. Especially, considering the increasing disparity between the poor and the rich in China, communism seems too far to approach.

> Some students have doubts about communism because they see the growing gap between the poor and the rich. A friend of my mother's has been laid-off. She lives on one hundred RMB per month. My mother's salary is only five hundred RMB each month. While window-shopping, I saw some ladies buying dresses that cost over 500 RMB each. They spent that much money without any hesitation. I feel poor walking in the crowd.

After 50 years of socialist reconstruction, the general living standards of the Chinese people have improved. But the distribution of wealth in Chinese society has become increasingly unequal and disproportionate. To these students, China seemed even further from the ideal of communist society than before. There is little wonder why the students did not believe in the coming of communism.

Another three interviewees do not believe in communism because of their doubts concerning the theoretical foundation of communist ideology. One student concludes, "I don't think communism will be realized. I doubt communism is the highest stage of human society. Maybe there is something else even better. It is impossible to have a system without private property." Another student says, "The evolvement of human society won't stop because of communism…the world is material and is constantly in motion." Still another suggests, "Human society may develop in a different direction. Another system may be the best and the ultimate."

The current study confirms the extensive ideological disillusionment present in post-Mao China, which has been termed "China's core problem" (Link 1994:189). It helps us to understand the extent to which the students have lost their confidence in communist ideology.

Thirdly, it is striking that almost one-third (31 percent) of the questionnaire respondents believe in communism. Fortunately, the in-depth interviews again provide insights for understanding this attitude. Although 8 out of the 21 interviewees suggested communism would eventually come true in China, a careful analysis reveals that not all of them have a strong faith in it. Half of them believe communist society is the natural result of social evolution. As one student states, "I think communism will come true.

It is the inevitable result of social evolution. This is the natural law for human society."

However, for the other half the coming of communism represents the fulfillment of a personal wish rather than the result of natural law. As one student says, "Living in a socialist country, it is my wish to see communism come true."

Another student explains,

> We have been taught communism since we were little. We hear it all the time. I think it is idealistic. It is a wish. We all hope for something beautiful. Maybe that is why some of us still believe in communism. But nowadays China is constructing a market economy. Communism seems further away.

In conclusion, students' attitudes towards the communist ideal vary. The majority of them do not have a strong faith in communism. Some of them do not believe communism will come true; some are indifferent to this issue; and some consider it just a beautiful dream.

## The Taught Moral Curriculum

In accordance with Cuban's (1992) curriculum typology, while the intended moral curriculum consists of the values and ideology the government expects to be taught, the taught curriculum is what the school and teachers actually do and use to present the officially intended values and ideology. In the taught curriculum the school and the teachers' own beliefs, ideals and agendas are infused into the intended curriculum. Cuban also suggests that it is the informal side of the taught curriculum, also called the hidden curriculum that often alters the intended or explicit curriculum.

This study provides evidence of the negative influences of the hidden curriculum on students' school experiences. It finds that students at Central High School respond rather negatively toward the school's implementation of the intended or explicit moral curriculum. It also reveals that both the school and the teachers pursue their own agendas while carrying out the intended or explicit curriculum, which undermine the purpose of the intended moral curriculum.

According to Cuban's (1992) theory, the hidden curriculum exists both at the level of the school and at the level of the teachers. Both the school and the teachers infuse their beliefs and ideals into their implementation of the intended curriculum. This study finds that students respond rather negatively to how the officially intended moral education curriculum is implemented at Central High School. In particular, it finds that students have many complaints about how the campaign of learning from Lei Feng is conducted and how their moral conduct is evaluated.

## The Campaign of Learning from Lei Feng

The campaign of learning from Lei Feng is an important part of the officially intended moral curriculum. However, the study reveals that the school incorporates its own agenda into the process of carrying out the campaign of learning from Lei Feng. Lei Feng, the long established moral model, is considered the highest manifestation of collectivism (J. Lin 1993; Reed 1991; Wu 1992; Zhang and Lu 1996). Lei Feng was a soldier of the People's Liberation Army who died in an accident in 1962 at the age of 22. Lei Feng was described as a perfect human being and an ideal communist soldier. According to the propaganda, Lei Feng consciously studied Mao's works and followed Mao's directives; he obeyed all arrangements by the Party; he was selfless and helped others with his whole heart; he lived a plain life but sent money he saved to those devastated by floods. Lei Feng was considered flawless.

After Lei Feng's death, a nationwide campaign of Learning from Lei Feng was launched. The campaign was extremely influential in the early 1960s, especially among youth and children. The spirit of Lei Feng was brought up again in the 1990s in a campaign emphasizing Lei Feng's loyalty to the Party, commitment to socialism, giving to instead of taking from society, and serving the people with the whole heart (Zhang and Lu 1996).

Like all other Chinese schools, Central High School has organized activities for students to learn from Lei Feng. Although learning from Lei Feng is a year-long program, March is called the Month of Learning from Lei Feng, dedicated to special activities to honor Lei Feng. Various projects are undertaken by the Communist Youth League and the Young Pioneer production brigade. In addition, every student in the school is involved in activities such as cleaning the riverbank in the city and cleaning bicycles for teachers.

This study finds that not all of the interviewees think highly of the campaign of learning from Lei Feng. Some students suggest that the learning from Lei Feng campaign is a hypocritical business. One of them says that the campaign seems political in nature rather than aimed at fostering moral character and it does not truly reflect Lei Feng's spirit. Another student complains, "There were too much empty talks but little actions in learning from Lei Feng." Still another student points out that learning from Lei Feng has become the observance of an annual occasion instead of being part of their everyday life.

The spirit of Lei Feng is never out of date but the method used to learn from Lei Feng is not good. It is like observing a festival. March 3rd is the "Day of Learning from Lei Feng." After that day there is no more learning from Lei Feng.

Furthermore, some students suggest that the campaign of learning from Lei Feng is like putting on a show. One student says,

> It is like putting on a show. They usually do not clean the school like that because it isn't a big deal if the school is not clean. Learning from Lei Feng like this is only an act of formality. It is of no use. Organize a group to clean up and then another group comes to make a mess.

According to this student, the campaign of learning from Lie Feng at Central High School becomes an obligation for the school. In order to maintain its status with the Educational Committee, the school has to fulfill the requirements of learning from Lei Feng.

The same student continues,

> The Student Association cleaned the bicycles for all the teachers on Lei Feng's Day. All the Youth League members went to clean the streets. It is just like our head teacher sending several students to clean the bicycles for the female teachers on Women's Day. Many students had a bad attitude while doing it. This is all about Lei Feng's Day. The nature of learning from Lei Feng has been changed. It should be part of our life. But it is instead an assigned task.

It seems to many students that the activities of learning from Lei Feng are imposed on them. As one student points out, they are not given the choice to decide for themselves what kind of activities they want to participate in.

> Learning from Lei Feng has become a laughing stock because it is not done out of willingness and spontaneity, but forced by the school. I think we should do it out of our free will and start with things around us. It can be small things, not necessarily cleaning the fences in the street...I think

the school should let the students decide what kind of good deeds they want to do instead of making the arrangement for them.

This student prefers doing good deeds spontaneously. It is common that students are reluctant to do the activities that they feel are imposed on them. They want to be given opportunities to express themselves in the process of learning from Lei Feng.

In conclusion, the study reveals that the students at Central High School are not interested in participating in the learning from Lei Feng campaign. Though the government intends to promote a loyalty to the Party, a love of socialism, a sacrificial spirit, and a love of service at the school level through the Lei Feng campaign (Zhang and Lu 1996), students believe the campaign was reduced to a forced, superficial, and short-lived event of street sweeping and bicycle cleaning.

This study finds that although the government has recently emphasized student-centered moral education in order to produce a labor force that possesses initiative and is independent-minded, moral education practice at Central High School still clings to the traditional model. This finding supports Lee's (1996) argument that there is a disparity between the official moral education policy promulgated by the central government and the practice of moral education at the local school level.

## The Scoring System of Conduct

Besides the campaign of learning from Lei Feng, the evaluation of student conduct is another issue that students complain about. According to the school regulations, a student gains 60 points if he/she observes the rules for secondary school students (SEC 1998e). However, it is the observance of the school-made rules that determines the students' conduct scores. These school-made rules are largely related to studying behavior and gaining publicity for the school. For example, the five-presences require that students involve their mind, eyes, ears, mouth, and hands in classroom learning; and those students who have become famous will have their photo displayed and will be treated as heroes of the school. Absence from class will result in a loss of 1 point and *zaolian* (too early love) will lead to a monthly deduction of 2–5 points. Winning awards at different levels, such as provincial, city, district, and school levels will score 4, 3, 2 and 1 points respectively.

According to the in-depth interviews, the scoring system is not cultivating moral character, but encouraging wrong motives for good behaviors. In a group interview of 5 students, 4 students suggest that this system is flawed because it can only evaluate students outward behaviors. One student says, he method is not helpful for cultivating students morality. A student with bad conduct can score high if he is not caught by the teachers. Another student states, he mathematical calculation of students morality and conduct is wrong. Students do good deeds in order to get good scores for their own benefit Most people do good deeds only to increase their scores.

Another student suggests, "The conduct measurement is helpful in restraining students from doing wrong. But it can be taken advantage of. Some students do good deeds in order to get the points. They ask for points immediately after doing something good."

One student even argues that such a scoring method commercialized moral education. According to him, moral character is treated as a commodity under the scoring system because moral character can be bought with outward behaviors. Only one student suggests the scoring method is useful as a threat. It serves as a constraint and thus reduces behavior problems among the students.

Students' negative attitudes find support in teachers' responses to the idea of quantifying moral conduct. In an interview with 5 class masters, they agree that this method is not useful at all. One class master concludes,

> Scores cannot truly reflect the conduct of a student. For example, a good student may forget to bring in homework once in a while. It is not a big deal. Li Ping (pseudonym) is striving to do as many good deeds as possible right now. He says he wants to gain more points to make up for the points he has lost. Some students score many points but lose many points too. Some students gain a few but lose a few too. The scoring system is only one method of supervising students. It serves as a kind of threat.

Another class master says he does not use this system at all. He says that his class is a slow class. The students do not care whether they gain or lose points. They know it will not matter. An employer will not look at their conduct scores and the teacher's evaluation when they go out to find a job.

In conclusion, this study finds that students respond negatively toward the scoring system of moral conduct. The students believe that the scoring system is not an effective method of evaluating conduct. It is flawed because it overemphasizes outward behaviors and encourages the wrong motives for doing good deeds.

## The Competitive Classroom Environment

The overall school culture at Central High School is academic-oriented rather than character-oriented. It is a common practice for Chinese secondary schools to group students into two categories: the humanities class and the science class. This is because the students of humanities and science study different subjects that are tested on the national college entrance exam. However, the senior three students at Central High School are instead grouped into an advanced class and a slow class. Both the advanced class and the slow class have students studying humanities and science. The advanced class has the best teachers in both humanities and science while the slow class finds itself in a disadvantaged situation. Although such classification of students complicates staffing and adminis-tration, the school leadership believes it makes the best use of the school's resources. In this way, the school hopes to ensure that the students in the advanced class pass the national college exam at the expense of the other students.

Furthermore, the students are subjected to transferring between classes based on their performance in several tests intended for this purpose. If a student in the advanced class does not do well, he/she will be put in the slow class. By the same token, a student in the slow class will be promoted to the advanced class if his/her test score is high enough. Such a strategy creates fierce competition among the students. This strategy seriously undermines the teaching of collectivism in addition to potentially harming the self-esteem of the less-advanced students.

Five (5) of the interviewees share the experience of being transferred between the advanced class and the slow class, 3 of whom have been transferred several times. When asked about their experiences, they all expressed their dislike of the highly competitive atmosphere, especially in the advanced class. They do not want to return to the advanced class once they are moved to the slow class.

> I don't want to go back to the advanced class even if I do well enough in the next exam. I like my class now. Because we are friends. We help each other. In the advanced class everything is about competition. It is hard to find anyone who is sincere. Everything is under the table. They attack each other from behind. It is depressing.

The pressure of academic competition makes it difficult for students to be collective-minded. The students become less interested in collective activities. As a class master says, today's students do not want to be together for occasions as a class collective. According to her, her students in the past loved to have a party to celebrate the New Year together. But her students at the present time are not interested in having a New Year party as a class. They prefer being with their best friends. She feels a strong resistance from her class to hold this traditional occasion.

This finding supports Thogerson's (1990) observation on the negative impact of conflicting values on Chinese secondary school students. Collectivism is still promoted officially but the classroom is highly competitive, which makes it difficult for students to practice collectivism. When the competition for a spot in the advanced class and eventually a seat in a college classroom is so fierce, it is almost impossible for the students to help others in their collective.

In conclusion, the taught moral education curriculum at Central High School conveys values contradictory to the intended curriculum in various ways. Not only moral education activities and evaluation methods, but also management strategies such as the classification of students, can convey values and ideology contradicting those manifested in the intended moral curriculum.

It is obvious that Central High School is caught between the fierce competition of the market economy and the collective socialist morality they are supposed to teach. In order to survive in the highly competitive school market, the current school leadership has to make every effort to improve students' academic performance. Due to poor student resources and limited facilities, Central High School has to work extra hard to survive in the competition. Besides prolonged school hours and extended school days, the school creates a competitive learning environment. Although the consequences of promoting competitiveness are at odds with the regime-sponsored virtue of collectivism, the school has no other choice.

## Teaching in the Taught Curriculum

According to traditional Chinese thinking, teachers are not only responsible to teach knowledge but also to nurture the person. Teachers are expected to influence students through their moral strength and good conduct in addition to transmitting academic knowledge. The teacher as role model is regarded as highly important in moral teaching. According to the questionnaire, the majority of students (68 percent) at Central High School expect their teachers to be role models (see Table B-9, Appendix B).

However, the questionnaire reveals that only 41 percent of the students consider their teachers to be good role models (see Table B-10, Appendix B). In fact, the interviewees repeatedly stated that the generation before them, including the teachers, cannot serve as role models, because they were poorly educated in many ways during the turmoil of the Cultural Revolution. Several students point out that the reform of moral education should start with the moral character of moral education workers.

According to Cuban's (1992) curricula typology, the intended curriculum becomes taught curriculum when teachers put their beliefs and behaviors into their teaching. This study finds that it is common for teachers at Central High School to deliver a hidden curriculum that is inconsistent with the officially intended moral curriculum. The teachers' personal beliefs and conduct are infused into the taught moral curriculum through their interaction with the students within the classroom and beyond.

## Teachers' Values and Ideology

This study finds that not only the students but also some teachers at Central High School hold beliefs and values that are contradictory to the intended moral curriculum. Moreover, it is not uncommon for these teachers to convey unofficial values and ideology in their teaching.

According to a political course teacher, Politics, a formal course that explicitly teaches official ideology and values, is no long considered as a means of indoctrination; rather, it is treated as a mere subject which is required for the national college entrance examination.

Unofficial beliefs and ideas are not accepted in the Chinese school system, especially in subjects taught in the humanities. There is a standard answer for almost every question in humanities. Thus this system has created a dilemma for teachers who disagree with regime-sponsored values and ideology. This study reveals that teachers have developed a coping strategy by which they encourage their students to overtly support official values and ideology and conceal their opposition when taking exams.

One student states, "My Politics teacher says he agrees that the CCP is not good, but he says we cannot write this in the exams." Another student says, "Our class teacher says that we may think differently but we cannot speak out in exams."

The unofficial beliefs of the teachers can cause confusion among the students. However, teachers find themselves caught in this confusion as well. As a teacher at Central High School says, Political Economics in

Chinese secondary schools is intended to provide theoretical explanation and support for China's economic policy. However, the speed of the reform is so fast that the textbook cannot keep up with the changes. The frequent revisions of the textbook make it impossible for teachers to digest the fast-changing new materials. In addition, the current textbook lacks theoretical soundness. The teachers find that the newly constructed theories are not very convincing.

Like all other school courses, language arts are supposed to teach official values and ideology as prescribed in the intended curriculum. Therefore the topics of composition are loaded with values and ideology. A female student makes the following comments on the teaching of a Chinese language and literature course, which she believes is hypocritical.

> Chinese Language and Literature is my favorite subject. But I don't like composition because the topics given to us are meaningless. I cannot write about my real feelings. I have to make up things. For example, we have been asked to write on the topic A Meaningful Event many times in our school years. I have only lived ten something years and every day I go back and forth between school and home. I run out of things to write about. Plus there are certain things that I cannot write about... but if I do not write on the topics given to us I cannot get good scores... Our Chinese language and literature teacher gives us serious warnings. According to him, one student did not get a high score for his composition in the national college entrance exam because he did not present the official teaching. The required topic was How to Be a Good Person. He changed the topic into It's No Use to Be a Good Person.

The same female student states that this bold yet unlucky student does not believe in being a good person. He argues that being good will lead to being taken advantage of by others and will do him no good. According to the interviewee, although his argument is well developed and supported with evidence and examples, the exam reader fails him. Simply, unofficial beliefs cannot be accepted in exams. Students will be punished for presenting unofficial opinions in exams.

According to another student, his teacher suggested that students had to lie in order not to jeopardize good scores on exams.

> I disagree. Examiners shouldn't judge a composition by its ideology and fail a student for his negative statements about society. If a composition is well written it is a good composition regardless of its ideology... My

teacher says we should lie rather than state the truth if we were in such a situation.

It is worth noting that the hidden message behind such teaching is untruthfulness. Teachers encourage the students not to say what they believe but what they are supposed to believe. The outcome of this practice is that the students learn to conceal their ideas and beliefs for practical reasons. The same student continues,

> In the end, students become very superficial and hypocritical and they lack imagination in their writing... At one school, the students were asked to write on the topic, How I Overcome My Weakness or Perseverance: My Desired Character. All the students wrote that they were disabled and both parents were deceased. This is ironic.

In conclusion, teachers' unofficial beliefs and ideas are clearly revealed in their teaching and interaction with the students. Caught in the dilemma of preaching what they disagree with, teachers have to achieve a delicate balance between teaching what they believe is true and being responsible for the future welfare of their students. They want to uphold what is true. At the same time, they have to consider the possible consequences of such teaching for the future of their students. Sometimes, it is impossible to resolve the dilemma.

## Class Masters' Style and Conduct

According to Lo (2001), social expectations of class masters are especially high. Traditionally, class masters are considered role models and expected to have a high level of social commitment and responsibility. They are expected to be ethically exemplary and willing to serve and commit to educating the younger generation (Lo 2001).

Class masters are said to be an important channel for cultivating the desired ideology and character among the students and instructing them in their overall development (SEC 1998b). They are made "a paragon of virtue for students to follow" (Bakken 1991:133). They function as a combination of homeroom teacher and guidance counselor (Chan 1997).

However, considering the importance of class masters in moral teaching, it is ironic that few students believe that their class masters embody high moral character. According to the questionnaire, class masters are rated last concerning their moral character after scholars, communist models, parents, political leaders, and friends (see Table B-11, Appendix B).

The in-depth interviews with the students help explain such negative attitudes, shedding light on why students hold quite negative attitudes toward their class masters. Interviewees come from three different classes, each of which has a class master. Interviewees from one class reveal few opinions about their class master, suggesting they do not know him well because he just received his assignment as their class master. However, interviewees from the other two classes have much to say about their class masters. Interviewees from one of the two classes seem to complain more about their class master's management style while interviewees from the other class voice strong criticisms of their class master as a person.

The first class master is in her late 40s. Her class is an advanced class. She teaches Language and Literature to her class. She has many years of work experience as a class master and she has been awarded the title of Excellent Class Master. Her devotion to her job can be seen through her long working hours at school and consistently close supervision of her students. Her class is more disciplined and has less behavioral problems when compared with other classes. The students are comparatively more motivated and cooperative. In order to ensure a good learning environment, she has even risked her health by scheduling her long-delayed surgery during the school sports meet when all classes were cancelled. She was back with her students before she was fully recovered.

One would think that her students would feel lucky to have her as class master. However, this study finds that in general her students do not appreciate her devotion and hard work. A common complaint heard in the in-depth interviews is that she is too controlling. Before she left for the hospital, she left an assignment for her class, which was a journal entry, "While the head teacher is not in ..." The metaphor of cat and rat repeatedly appears in students' responses.

As one student writes,

Our class master is like the cat. The students are like the rats. When the cat is away, the rats become wild... When she is around, she likes spying on us. It makes us feel as if we were doing something underground—we have to hold our breath. Since she went into the hospital, we are liberated. It is like the song which goes "The sky in the Liberated Region is blue; the people in the Liberated Region are glad..." Now we can walk keeping our heads up. We are no longer afraid of being attacked from behind... We are so happy.

The author of the above quote is not a problem student. Even the well-adjusted students have complaints, including those with titles of honor like *sanhao xuesheng* ("three-good student," referring to someone who is outstanding in ideological orientation, academic performance, and physical fitness). One "three-good student" says,

Teachers only pay attention to academics and ignore character...Teachers use the wrong methods in moral education. It's very hard for students to take. Teachers are not friendly. There are obstacles in the relationship between teachers and students.

As one of the top students in the class points out,

We don't like our head teacher. She is too strict and does not care for our self-respect. She is not nice... We hope teachers would be good role models for us. But my class teacher's words and actions are not consistent. The election of the class committee is not fair. But we dare not object.

This interviewee is a class committee member. She is very unhappy about how the class master handled the recent election of the class committee. According to her, the class master dismissed the election results and ordered another election. Apparently, the class master did not think the student with the most votes for the position of head of the class was the right person. So the class master just dismissed the election results, exclaiming, "Some of you are not serious about the election."

Only one female student gives somewhat positive feedback concerning her class master.

Our class master cares about us very much. She pays attention to our everyday well-being and our emotions. She engages the students in deep conversation, talking about their concerns and struggles. She is very good at persuasion... There were times when she upset some students because she criticized them in front of the whole class. Usually she would talk to the student privately afterward to explain why she had criticized him or her.

This girl is one of the few students from broken families in the entire school. Her parents are divorced and she alternately lives with her mother and father. She is in an advanced class yet her grades are not consistent due to her family situation. While other students feel the class master is too controlling, she appreciates the class master's concern for her and long talks with her. However, this student mentions that sometimes the head master humiliates students in front of the whole class.

There is a tension between what the students expect from their class master and how she does her job. Typical of teenagers, the students want more independence and less supervision. Also, they are influenced by western ideas. They are not in favor of the traditional authoritative style of the class master.

On the other hand, the class master strives to maintain control over her students and make sure they perform well academically. She is held responsible for student's test scores as well their overall well being. Her class is supposed to compete with students from other schools including key schools in the national college entrance exam. Due to the relatively poor academic performance and study habits of her students, the headmaster is under great pressure. It is essential for her to maintain control in order to create an environment in which students can focus on their studies and attain good scores. The student with the most votes in the first election is well liked by his fellow students but he tends to break rules sometimes. Apparently, the class master cannot risk having him as head of the class.

Another class master mentioned in the student in-depth interviews is a young man in his thirties. He is a physics teacher. He is the class master of a slow class. He teaches physics to both his own class and an advanced class. He spends most of his time preparing for his teaching assignment instead of his class master job. In contrast to the other class master, he does not spend much time supervising his class. He states in an interview, "I don't have much time for that. I have a heavy teaching load. I let the students supervise themselves." Indeed, he hardly comes to the classroom except for his teaching assignment or to make announcements.

According to the in-depth interviews, there is a great distaste for this class master among the students. The students use strong words to describe him, such as "disgusting," "ugly," "immoral," and "a persecutor."

It is believed that the students' negative attitudes toward him have something to do with his perception of the students and how he relates to them. Despite their poor test scores and challenging behaviors, these students are active and athletic. In fact they have won the most medals in the school sports meets. Some of them are very bright. However, in an interview that took place in his office, this class master refers to his students as *zhazi* (waste), which means they are undesired materials left in the filtering process of the competitive educational system. According to him, these students are ruined by poor parenting and bad influences from society. They are not disciplined and they have no motivation for anything.

This study finds that the negative feelings are mutual between the class master and his students. The students consider him a poor teacher and a person without integrity. One student states,

> My class teacher is not a nice person. He does not respect students. He is not caring. He damages students' self-esteem. He is not reliable or responsible. Yesterday, he asked a student to answer a question. The student gave the right answer in a soft voice, but the teacher did not hear it. The teacher asked the student to repeat the answer. And this time the student changed his answer into a wrong one. The teacher said to him, "You might as well give up and quit school." The other day he saw a student work really hard in the general cleaning. He said to the student, "Why are you working so hard? You take it too serious." His facial expressions are very unpleasant. Many students change their major from science to humanities in order to avoid looking at his face.

Many students complain that the class master treats them in an insensitive and even humiliating manner. His attitude towards his students has become so unbearable for many students that they try in every way to avoid him. As another student says,

> I am so disgusted with him that I cannot make myself look at him every day. That is why I choose to study humanities instead of science. I don't have to attend the physics class he is teaching... The reality is so cruel. One can become *toupuoxueliu* (black and blue all over).

This male student is very bright, yet defiant. For example, he does not want to have his hair cut really short as required. He always gets himself in trouble, including being moved to a slow class. Usually, students who study science are considered to have a better career path than those who study humanities. This boy can do well in science but he has chosen to study humanities instead of science in order to avoid his class master. His experience with his class master at school affects his entire outlook on life.

Another student observes,

> Some teachers are good role models but some are not. My class teacher in the elementary school was a model teacher and she taught us how to be a good person. But my current class teacher has persecuted me for the past three years. He thinks he has the right to do wrong just because he is the teacher. He never admits his mistakes nor apologizes. He does not listen to students' opinions.

This student is currently head of the class. Apparently, her experience working with the class master as a leader of the class has been very unpleasant. The least negative feedback about him is from a female student who has been transferred between the advanced and slow class several times. "I have little contact with my class master. I don't want to speak to him, and I don't have anything to say to him."

It is likely that the students overstate their negative feelings toward their class master. However, it is evident that there are serious problems in the relationship between the class master and his students. It is understandable that the students may become angry with their class master who considers them to be rubbish.

Looking at their interaction from a student perspective, it seems that this class master is simply a bad person. However, the situation is more complicated than it might seem. It is believed that the class master is in a very difficult situation. In order to increase academic performance, the school grouped the more advanced students in one class and the rest in another class. This class master reluctantly watched good students pulled out of his class and poor students placed in his class. Because it is a slow class, everybody knows that none of the students will likely pass the national college entrance exam.

In an exam-oriented environment, it is not rewarding for a teacher to teach a class in which none of the students are likely to pass the national exam and go on to college. Moreover, it is much more difficult to be a class master for a class made up of students with behavior problems and poor motivation. Besides, because a teacher's compensation and benefits are tied to the academic performance of his students, this assignment is not to his financial advantage. As this headmaster mentions, he is not as fortunate as some of his college classmates who are teaching at key schools. They have high-achieving students, few behavioral problems to deal with, and better compensation. It is fair to say that teachers can become victimized in the current school system.

It is evident that the majority of students at Central High School respond very negatively toward their teachers, especially their class masters. Although teachers are officially considered the most important channel of moral education, the students do not think highly of them. There is a sharp contrast between the students' high expectations of teachers as role models and their disappointment about some teachers' problematic performance as observed in their school experiences.

It is worth noting that negative attitudes toward teachers are not only an issue among the problem students who are more likely to have conflicts with their teachers. The well-adjusted students also have complaints. Some students do not like their class master's authoritative style. Other students complain about their class master's insensitivity and neglect.

In conclusion, it is evident that the school and teachers infuse their own agendas and beliefs in the implementation of the intended moral curriculum. Within the competitive school system and market economy, the school and teachers focus on students' academic performance while overlooking the cultivation of official ideology and values. Moral education practices are found to be problematic at both the administration level and the teacher level. There is a large gap between what the government intends to achieve through the moral education curriculum and what is actually taught in the classroom.

# 6

## THE IMPACT OF THE ECOLOGICAL ENVIRONMENT

As discussed in the previous chapter, students at Central High School hold very negative attitudes toward the moral education curriculum. Students respond negatively towards both the officially intended moral curriculum and the hidden moral curriculum. In this chapter, Bronfenbrenner's (1979) ecological theory of human development will be used as the framework for discussing the extent to which the ecological environment helps shape the formation of such negative attitudes in students.

## Ecological Theory of Human Development

According to Urie Bronfenbrenner (1979), development is the continuous process in which a developing person interacts with his environment, which he describes as a set of interconnected structures at different levels. At the innermost level is the microsystem (Bronfenbrenner 1979), the immediate setting of the developing person, such as school and home. The next level is the mesosystem, the interconnection between the immediate settings. Then comes the exosystem, the interconnection between the settings that the developing person may never enter but that nevertheless affect the developing person indirectly. The macrosystem is the overarching pattern of ideology and belief systems common to the particular culture or society. Smith, Cowie and Blades (1998:11) well explain Bronfenbrenner's theory in a diagram of nested circles (see Fig. 2).

Besides the concept of nested environment, interconnection is another essential concept in Bronfenbrenner's (1979) ecological theory. The interconnections among other persons in the immediate setting, as well as those among settings at different levels, are regarded as important as the objects and people that the developing person interacts with face to face. The core of ecological theory is the concern with the progressive accommodation between a growing human organism and its immediate environment, and the way in which this relation is mediated by forces emanating from more remote regions in the larger physical and social milieu. The ecology of human development lies at a point of convergence among the disciplines of the biological, psychological and social sciences as they bear on the evolution of the individual in society.

Thus, Bronfenbrenner's (1979) ecological theory not only provides a scheme for detecting wide-ranging environmental influences, but also offers a systematic structure for analyzing the interplay among these settings. Ecological theory was originally designed as a framework for analyzing environmental factors in relation to human psychological and behavioral development. However, ecological theory has greatly influenced educational policy in America, for example, the establishment of Head Start, a nation-wide program that provides early education to children from disadvantaged families. This study extends human ecological theory to the field of moral education.

While exploring the students' attitudes toward the moral education curriculum, this study attempts to understand the environmental factors at different ecological levels and their role in shaping such attitudes. For example, at the microsystem level, this study will look at how activities and dynamics within the school influence students' attitudes toward the moral education curriculum. At the exosystem level, the impact of the conflicts between social realities and school moral and ideological teachings will be examined. The changes in national economic policy in general and the changes in parent's employment in particular are considered important factors that shape student's attitudes at the mesosystem level. The reform ideology and changing values in Chinese society at the macrosystem level also play a part in the formation of student's attitudes towards the moral education curriculum.

Interconnection is an important principle of ecological theory. According to Bronfenbrenner (1979), the course of human development is not an isolated process but the result of the interactions of settings at different levels. The developmental potential of a person is enhanced when settings at different levels are compatible with mutually positive feelings, consented goals, and supportive activities. Conversely, without these elements, the developmental potential of the person is impaired.

In accordance with ecological theory, the Central High School students' process of moral learning can been seen as an interplay between students and their ecological environment at different levels, namely, school, and the links between school and home, social realities, and the overarching belief system of the society. The present chapter will discuss how basic elements in the school setting and the interconnection between settings affect the adoption of official values, ideology, and conduct among the students. In accordance with the interconnection principle, the developing students, the environment, the structure of environmental settings, and the processes taking place within and between them will be viewed as interdependent and will be analyzed in systems terms (Bronfenbrenner 1979).

## School as Developmental Context

In accordance with ecological theory, school is an immediate setting in the students' development, the so-called microsystem. According to Bronfenbrenner, a microsystem is "a pattern of activities, roles, and interpersonal relations experienced by the developing person in a given setting with particular physical and material characteristics" (Bronfenbrenner 1979:22). The school environment of Central High School, especially the dynamics of its smallest functional unit, class, will be examined as a developmental context. According to Bronfenbrenner, activities, roles, and interpersonal structure are the three basic elements of a setting. In this study, each of these three elements will be discussed in terms of its impact on students' experience of moral learning at Central High School.

## Activities

According to Bronfenbrenner, the milieu of social activity has great potential to influence human development. "The developmental status of the individual is reflected in the substantive variety and structural complexity of the molar activities which she initiates and maintains in the absence of instigation or direction by others" (1979:55).

Soviet educators use play, fantasy, and games primarily to develop communist morality, which represents a high level of social conformity and submission to authority. Play, fantasy, and games can just as effectively be utilized to develop initiative, independence, and equalitarianism (Bronfenbrenner 1979).

At Central High School, the learning from Lei Feng campaign involves non-academic activities though, due to the school's examination orientation and emphasis on test scores, it does not encourage play and fantasy. Students are organized to do good deeds during *xue Lei Feng yue* (the month of learning from Lei Feng). However, according to student interviews, these activities are not helpful for internalizing the Lei Feng spirit. The students are found to be either indifferent or resistant to such activities.

It is believed that these activities lack variety and complexity, which are crucial to internalizing the intended values and ideology. Every year the students are asked to do tasks such as cleaning the riverbank, sweeping streets and cleaning bikes for teachers. The students do not consider these activities helpful for developing Lei Feng's spirit. Rather, they are considered to be only for show and meaningless. The streets get littered and dusty shortly thereafter, but it does not seem important to those who initiate the activity.

As a non-key school with less competent students and limited resources, it is a difficult task for Central High to survive in the competitive market economy. In order to improve its academic record and attract more funding, the school has to focus on academic teaching. The campaign of learning from Lei Feng is definitely not the priority of the school. The school feels obliged to fulfill the activity requirement of learning from Lei Feng. However, the consequences and the effect of these activities are not its major concerns. Therefore, it is reasonable to believe that the over-emphasis on test scores of the competitive school system is to be blamed. The competitive system is thought to be largely responsible for the fact that the learning from Lei Feng campaign at the school level becomes a matter of formality.

According to Bronfenbrenner (1979), the initiation of the developing individual in activities is crucial for the development of the individual. It is believed that, besides the lack of substantive variety and structural complexity in the activities of learning from Lei Feng, there is an absence of student initiation. In the interviews, students commonly complain that they do not have a chance to decide which activities they prefer for learning from Lei Feng. They suggest that they are not motivated to do those activities assigned to them.

Thus, the activities organized in the learning from Lei Feng campaign lack variety, complexity and a spontaneous nature. These activities become a kind of formality. They do not facilitate student learning and development.

## Interpersonal Structures

According to Bronfenbrenner, the interpersonal structure of a setting is a crucial part of an individual's process of learning and development. Reciprocity, balance of power and affective relation are important properties of interpersonal structure.

Learning and development are facilitated by the participation of the developing person in progressively more complex patterns of reciprocal activity with someone with whom that person has developed a strong and enduring emotional attachment and when the balance of power gradually shifts in favor of the developing person (1979:60).

The most favorable situation for a developing person is one in which alance of power gradually shifts in favor of the developing person, in other words, when the latter is given increasing opportunity to exercise control over the situation (Bronfenbrenner 1979:58).

Unfortunately, the power relation between teacher and students at Central High School creates an unfavorable situation for students moral learning and development. Teachers, especially class masters, tend to be authoritative in their class management style. The students consider themselves to be powerless because their future depends on their teachers evaluation.

As in the event of the class election discussed in the previous chapter, the class master negated the election results in a seriously conducted class election. The class master apparently did not think the elected class monitor appropriate for the position. She simply ordered a reelection. As revealed in the students in-depth interviews, many students were upset with the class master action. However, none of the students dared to raise any objection.

Traditionally, Chinese classrooms are authoritative. Teachers have authority over students. Due to the current over-emphasis on test scores, teachers control of the classroom becomes more important. In order to create a good learning environment, teachers have to be strict with rules and discipline those students whose behavior interrupts classroom teaching and learning activities. It is reasonable that class masters want to have trustworthy class monitors who help supervise fellow students while teachers are not around. However, today students are more free-spirited and independent-minded. The traditional authoritative style of management is not well received among the students. Rather, it causes students negative attitudes toward their class masters.

In addition to the teachers' authoritative dominance, negative feelings between teachers and students also hinder students' adoption of the official ideology and values at Central High School. According to Bronfenbrenner (1979), development and learning will be enhanced if activities take place in a context characterized by mutuality of positive feeling. In other words, one learns more from a teacher with whom one has a close relationship. Conversely, mutual antagonism is especially disruptive of activities and interferes with learning.

As discussed in the previous chapter, the in-depth interviews reveal there is not a good relationship between class masters and their students. For example, one class master treats his class as "waste" in the competitive educational system while his class describes him with words such as "disgusting," "ugly," "tyrant," "immoral," and "persecutor."

Such mutual antagonism is largely a result of the categorization of students and the distribution of educational resources. Those students in non-key schools and slow classes are deprived of competent teaching and sufficient attention from teachers. They become less motivated and have more behavioral problems. As a result, those teachers reluctantly assigned to teach slow classes have a challenging yet not rewarding job. They tend to become indifferent and sometimes negligent toward their job and their students. On the other hand, the students feel abandoned and mistreated. Such a bad cycle is harmful for students' moral learning.

In conclusion, the problematic interpersonal structure within the school largely undermines the effectiveness of the intended moral curriculum. Students lack the opportunity to exercise power over the situation. There is also a lack of mutual positive feeling between students and teachers. The resulting teacher-student relationship does not facilitate learning and development; rather, it is disruptive and interferes with implementation of the moral curriculum.

## Role Expectations

According to Bronfenbrenner, a role is "a set of activities and relations expected of a person occupying a particular position in society, and of others in relation to that person" (Bronfenbrenner 1979:85). The concept of role involves an integration of the elements of activity and relation in terms of societal expectations. Role expectations are associated with every position in society.

As Bronfenbrenner (1979) observes, while it functions as an element of the microsystem, a role is rooted in the higher-order macrosystem. This is because role expectations are defined at the level of the subculture or culture as a whole and are associated with ideology and institutional structures. Therefore, role expectations have a special power to influence and even compel how a person behaves in a given situation, the activities engaged in and the relations established between that person and others present in the setting.

Bronfenbrenner suggests that the social expectation for teachers can vary from culture to culture. In modern Western societies, although both teacher and parent are expected to provide guidance to the young, the degree of reciprocity and mutual affection is presumed to be higher with parents than with teachers. Parental authority is thought to extend over a broader segment of the child's life than the teacher's (1979).

Social expectation of teachers is much higher in China than in modern Western societies. In traditional China, teachers were considered role models and examples of virtue. Even today, the social expectation of teachers has not changed. It is evident that the students at Central High School still expect their teachers to be role models with good character and moral behavior. However, these students are extremely disappointed by the poor modeling of their teachers. As revealed in the in-depth interviews, the teachers' poor conduct does not meet their students' expectations.

A majority of the teachers are considered to be poor role models by their students. Not that some teachers are not teaching about morality, but that they are contradicting the very moral curriculum they teach. Indeed, this practice demoralizes the intended moral curriculum and contributes to the students' indifference or distaste.

In addition, teachers' expectations for students also play an important part. Teachers have higher expectations for some students than for others. For example, students in a slow class are not expected to perform well in exams and go on to colleges and universities. Yet the students in an advanced class are expected to study hard and pass the national college entrance examination. Such differing expectations for students yield quite different consequences.

Though the advanced-class students receive close supervision, the slow-class students receive little supervision. Though the advanced-class students feel they are being oppressed in their highly competitive and controlled environment, the slow-class students feel abandoned due to laxity and inattention. Though the advanced-class students tend to be more focused, the slow-class students tend to have more discipline problems. However, both groups of students believe that character or moral learning is not considered a primary task at school.

Setting appropriate expectations for students is an important factor in facilitating learning and development. Unfortunately, Central High School does not make moral character or conduct a primary expectation for the students as a result of their survival strategy in the market economy. Thus the role expectation for students is detrimental to the moral learning and development of the students.

In conclusion, Central High School does not provide a favorable setting for students' adoption of the officially desired ideology and values in terms of activities, interpersonal relations and role expectations. Moral learning activities lack variety, complexity and student initiation. There is no mutual positive feeling between teachers and students and the latter have no sense of control over moral learning. The role expectations of students are problematic and teachers are not believed to model good character and moral behavior.

## Contexts Beyond the School

According to the ecological theory, the developmental potential of a person is enhanced when settings at different levels are found compatible with mutually positive feelings, consented goals, and supportive activities. The developmental potential of the person is impaired when these elements are lacking.

In accordance with the interconnection principle of the ecological theory, the effectiveness of the moral curriculum at Central High School is largely impaired by the incompatibility of settings at different levels. There are conflicts between these settings in terms of their goals, content, and strategies for moral learning. There is a lack of mutual positive feeling, consented goals, and supportive activities among these settings. These settings do not support each other but instead undermine each other in the moral learning process.

## Official Teachings vs. Social Realities

There is a clash between the official content of the moral curriculum and the surrounding social realities (Thogerson 1990). China is undergoing a radical transformation from an agricultural society to an industrial society, from an isolated society to an increasingly open society, from a socialist planned-economy to a capitalist market economy (Prybyla 1996). Chinese society has changed, yet the textbooks used at school have not changed much since the reform period.

As a teacher at Central High School observes, the course in political economy in Chinese secondary schools is intended to provide theoretical explanation and support to the reform policy under the leadership of the CCP. However, the speed of the reform is so fast that the textbooks cannot keep up with the changes. Therefore, the discrepancy between the teaching of the textbook and the current policy is severe. As one interviewee points out,

Our textbooks are full of contradictions. I don't like it at all... Politics and political economy are particularly bad. There are so many things I cannot comprehend. It gives me a headache when I read the textbook and reflect on the society realities. For example, the textbook says capitalist production is exploitation, but state-owned production is not exploitation. I also have problems with other issues.

The textbooks have been revised several times on the issue of owner-ship in the socialist economic system. What the students learned in grade 10 and grade 11 is different from what they are learning now in grade 12. The rapid changes cause confusion and frustration among the students.

One student says,

I think some subjects are indoctrination, especially politics, Chinese language and literature, and history. They are telling the truth. For example, during the Japanese invasion, the Nationalists under Chang Kai-Shek contributed to the defeat of the Japanese. But our textbooks eliminate their efforts and achievements. In another example, our textbooks claim the current economic system is mainly socialist and state-owned; our teacher disagrees, saying, in fact, it is mainly a market economy, but he suggests we have to follow the textbook in exams. Sometimes, I am very troubled.

Another student states, "What they teach us at school stands in contradiction to what the society is... For example, the school teaches us to have integrity; but society functions largely by use of the backdoor. You cannot survive with the school teaching in reality." Backdoor means social connections, which is another way of saying corruption. Frequently, people have to bribe officials to get things done. Another student says,

> I think what we are taught at school contradicts what we see in society... The teachings on values, life and money are not meaningful, because most students hold different views from the textbook, especially on money. Everywhere in society, you cannot see the doctor or stay in the hospital if you have no money. I know a young girl who is studying nursing because she has a sick father who needs medical care but has no money.

The textbook opposes the worship of money, but the student observes that in society that money is the only thing that makes things happen. Clearly, viewed from the interconnection principle of the ecological theory, the conflicts between the official content of the moral curriculum and social realities play an important role in shaping students' attitudes.

## Impact of Economic Policies

It is fair to say that the changes in national economic policies are a major factor that raises doubts among the students and resistance toward the intended moral curriculum. According to the ecological theory, a person development is profoundly affected by events occurring in settings in which the person is not even present. The changes in national economic policies, especially parent employment conditions, plays an important part in the students attitudes toward the content of the moral curriculum.

As economic reform accelerated, especially after the official conceptualization of market socialism, many state enterprises could hardly survive due to their own inefficiency and competition from the private sector. In the early 1990s the Chinese government adopted a policy that allowed state-owned enterprises to go bankrupt. In the city where Central High School is located, the bankruptcy of state-owned enterprises had become severe by 1996. A large number of the state workers had lost their jobs and were suffering severe financial difficulties. Also, as Chinese society becomes increasingly market-driven, the state no longer takes responsibility for benefits such as housing and medical care.

The majority of parents of the students at Central High School work for the state sector, which generally provides less compensation than the private sector. Moreover, many of the parents were reported to have been laid-off from their state jobs or expect to be laid-off soon. That is to say, many of the students' families are suffering financial losses from the economic policy changes.

The unemployment of their parents has caused many students at Central High School to doubt and resist communist ideals and question the purported superiority of socialism over capitalism. One student, whose mother lost her job in a state-owned company, writes the following,

> My mother lost her job... Every day she will get up about 4 o'clock in the morning to buy vegetables from the dealers and sell them in the market. She doesn't get home until late, about 7 o'clock at night. She works so hard, but she only makes about 300 *yuan* (equivalent to about 40 U.S. dollars) a month... I don't think communism will ever come true in China. Chinese socialism is still at its beginning stages. Communism is too far away.

Clearly, this student feels the negative consequences of reform. From her mother's experience she has developed serious doubts about the communist ideal. Another student says,

As for Deng and Jiang, people do not have a good impression of them because they made a mess in the country's economy. Many people lost their jobs, and the disparity between the poor and the rich is severe. I know a family of three who lives on $160 per month. Many of my relatives are affected by the bad economy. I also saw a TV program on poor families. My mother says even in Mao's time, life was easier for the poor.

Doubts and resistance are not the sole province of students whose parents have lost their state jobs. Those students whose parents are not affected by the policy changes also question the socialist ideology. They reflect on their observation of those who are less fortunate. A student, whose father is a self-employed taxi driver, states,

> I was never close to my father. We can talk to each other about social issues, but not personal issues. The other day my father told me he saw many factory workers protesting. The workers had worked for the factory all their lives. They have been used in the past and now they are kicked out just like that. This is so-called socialism... The head of the factory can lay off the workers. How come he never gets laid-off? I doubt the workers are owners of the country.

According to socialism, workers are said to own the country. In fact, as Mao stated, the workers make up the leading class of Chinese society. This student is challenging the orthodoxy of socialism. What he learned from the society, in this case through his father, contradicts the teaching at school. The workers have no say in management and have to leave when not needed. They are mere laborers rather than owners of the collective as they are said to be.

In addition, the increasing disparity between the poor and the rich in China since the reform period has become a hurdle to many students in relation to their belief in communism. As one student explains,

Some students have doubts about communism because they see the growing gap between the poor and the rich. A friend of my mother's has been laid-off. She lives on one hundred RMB per month. My mother's salary is only five hundred RMB ($65) each month. One day I was window-shopping. I saw some ladies buying dresses that cost over five hundred RMB each. They spent that much money without any hesitation. Walking in the crowd, I feel poor.

After 50 years of socialist reconstruction, the general living standards of the Chinese people have improved, but the distribution of wealth in Chinese society has become increasingly unequal and disproportionate to individuals' contributions. China seems even further from the idealistic communist society in which abundant wealth is equally distributed based on each person's need. Within such an environment, it is hard for the students to believe that socialism is better than capitalism and that communism will ultimately be realized in China. It is a common saying among the students at Central High School that school preaching is empty and not convincing.

In conclusion, the findings of the current study support Bronfenbrenner's (1979) ecological theory. The social settings that do not directly affect the students nonetheless influence their attitudes toward the moral education curriculum. Students' attitudes are affected by national economic policy, especially as it is manifested in parents' employment conditions.

## Impact of Media

The increasingly open Chinese cultural market plays an important role in conveying values and ideology contradictory to what the school preaches. According to Bronfenbrenner (1979), media serves as an important agent to bring the outside world into the developing individual's own world. The events outside their immediate setting thus impact the individual indirectly through a variety of media channels.

According to the student questionnaire data, many students consider media to be their major information source. When asked about the information channels they use most often, 87 percent of the students choose TV and movies; 86.5 percent of the students choose newspapers; 60 percent choose other people; 57 percent choose magazines; and 53 percent choose books. Only 39 percent of the students mention teachers as their information source. A negligible 2 percent of the students report the Internet as their information source (see Table B-12, Appendix B).

Clearly, a majority of students don't rely on their teachers for information, rather, they learn about the world around them through media, especially from TV, movies, and newspapers. This finding is supported by a national survey, in which 92 percent of the students' families have TV and watching TV is the primary cultural activity accounting for more than half of all leisure time (CCPCC and Central Institute for Educational Research 1990).

The influence of media is also a repeated theme in the interview narratives of the students at Central High School. It is evident that media, especially TV, movies and newspapers have a much deeper impact on the students than their school moral curriculum.

Media has contributed to the development of the current youth culture characterized by consumerism, independence and Western ethical standards. As Thogerson (1990) notes, a youth culture starts to appear during the 1980s when films, magazines, and TV introduced Western lifestyles to the younger generation and market mechanisms pushed publishing houses to print stories of sex and violence in order to increase their sales. The in-depth interviews reveal that many students at Central High School have abandoned the regime-sponsored values and ideology.

As one student observes,

> I think society has a bigger influence on students than school, especially media like TV, VCDs (video CDs) and newspapers. We learn a lot more from outside school... I enjoy my friends very much. We learn from each other about our studies, personalities and fashion styles. We all like good brands. We all like Nike, Reebok, Uright, and so on. My friends and I like the Back Street Boys and certain Hong Kong pop singers. I like cartoons from Japan and America, both science fiction and comedy... My father is the manager of a small store in his work unit. My mother works in a Chinese herb pharmacy. They didn't have much education and had a hard life during the Cultural Revolution. They live a very simple life... They lecture me about clothes and eating.

It is obvious that this generation is very different from their parents. They were born after the Cultural Revolution. They grew up during the reform period. They are exposed to Western movies and songs that convey modern values and concepts. As a result, there is a gap between this generation and their parents' generation concerning lifestyle and values.

The following narrative from another student reveals that media has something to do with the trend of more independent mindedness and self-awareness among youth.

I think society has a great influence on students through media, VCDs, TV and newspaper... I admire a life with freedom, less stress and more independence. I am not an adult yet. My parents are very strict with me. They give me many restrictions. They don't allow me to have a girlfriend. My father is in the architecture consulting business and he has been to America. I want to go to America too. I have many relatives living in America. I like movies that are less philosophical and more practical. I want to be independent. I like the Hong Kong romantic movie Everlasting Feelings. It is about commitment and adulthood. I also like the movie Air Force One. I don't think there is too much violence and sex in movies. We senior high students have a sense of right and wrong. But I know some students who rented pornographic VCDs for themselves.

This boy's desire for freedom and independence is typical of developmental characteristics of youth. What is more interesting is the way he relates his desires to the Western movies he enjoys watching. It is fair to say that these movies have great appeal for him because they promote the values he cherishes.

Another student directly credits the changes in sexual morality to media. "There was an open discussion in the newspaper about moving in together before getting married. I think it is OK based on what I learned on TV and in newspapers."

Another student feels overwhelmed by the impact of media. He strongly blames media for the changing moral values of youth.

I don't think moral education can be improved because the influence from outside society is too big...I think the influence of society is greater than parents, teachers or peer groups. Media is the most influential. There is lots of violence and pornography in the media. I read newspapers. My parents don't allow me to watch TV... Our generation is more diverse, more selfish, less ambitious, with less principles, and more open to sex. When our generation grows up, China will be the same as the Western countries—I mean in moral values. Divorce and living together before getting married is OK to most people. As for me? It depends. I have to consider other factors. Like housing.

It is clear that Western ethical standards and lifestyle are implanted into the students' minds through media. As this student points out, this generation shares the moral values of the youth in the West.

Media not only plays an important part in the spread of consumerism, independent-mindedness, and Western ethical standards among youth, it also undermines the school's efforts to instill socialist values such as collectivism. It is largely through media that students at Central High School find the official teachings taught at school to be contradictory to the social realities they live with. This section will discuss how media expose the students to such conflicts and thereby undermine the school's efforts to instill the regime-sponsored values.

I think school teaching is more effective for some students than for other students. Maybe half of the students have truly grasped collectivism and helping others. Some students may have learned a little. There are still some students who would endanger themselves to help others... I believe the influence of movies and TV on students is overwhelming. Ten times more influential. It takes only one movie or TV program to convince the students of something, but it will take a teacher saying the same thing ten times to convince them.

Almost every interviewee retells stories they learned through media. One student states,

The media is influential too. I like reading the newspaper, The West China Metropolitan. I read it every day. Action movies from Hong Kong are all about gangs. Students learn bad things such as robbery from the movies. The media emphasizes the dark side, such as TV programs about fake cigarettes, which are the most common cigarette on the market. Fake cigarettes are related to gangs. Students learn to falsify from these movies.

Another student says, "We learn different things from outside school. For example, I learned about a policeman. He was brave. But he lost his life in the line of duty. The onlookers wouldn't come to help him."

Another student points out,

Some of the worst influences come from society, like dishonesty and the profit-motive. For example, newspapers and TV falsely report profits.

They speak in favor of bad things if they are paid a great deal. A reporter dared to uncover a certain person's bad deeds and he was beaten to death...There are good things and bad things in the media. But it is the bad things that impress me more.

All these stories clearly capture the value conflicts in contemporary Chinese society. The students observe the low morals of the society and they conclude what the school preaches is not practical in everyday life. When asked if they would endanger themselves to help others, all interviewees but one answer no. One student says she would take a risk to help others under the condition that it brought fulfillment to her own life. Since she has not accomplished much, she cannot die young. Another student says she cannot because she has parents to take care of. Some students are afraid of retribution. Others say their parents will not allow them to. These responses may be typical of teenagers. Yet these responses clearly reveal that official values such as collectivism are not being successfully instilled among the students.

The in-depth interviews also suggest that students blame media for the increase in juvenile delinquency. All interviewees agree that the trouble-makers are just imitating what they learned from TV, movies and newspapers. As one student observes, "Media is very influential. There are lot of gunfights and kung fu on TV. Students watch it and try it out the very next day at school. They get into real fights often. It is most common in elementary school."

Another student says,

I think social influences are great. Especially on clothing, language, and ideology... There are good influences and bad influences. The bad influences are corruption and social activities such as gambling... Juvenile crime has increased. Some youth even use drugs. They watched it on TV and read in the newspaper. They want to try it out.

According to an interviewee, there is not a good system for censoring the cultural products available for youth in the media market.

Local TV stations often show pornography because of the loose censorship. Hong Kong movies showing gunfights and gangs have something to do with juvenile crime. For example, *Guhuozai* is all about gangs and violence. Many youth watch it several times. I watched it twice. The pirated VCDs, X-rated movies on CDs, are easy to find. The video shops would rent out to anybody, even children, to make money. Under the bridge near my home there are three different persons offering to sell me these CDs. That was within half a hour... I think most young people have been exposed to pornography. There are sex scenes in the gunfight movies. Those are the kinds of movies young people love to watch.

In addition, several interviewees blame the profit-driven media industry for its exaggeration of violence and pornography. One of them suggests,

> Media plays an important part in social life. I like the show Tonight 800 (a crime show). I don't like shows about celebrities. They produce idols for the student idol worshipers. Media exaggerates violence. For example, there was a news report on a murder. It gave every detail of the murder and how the body was dissolved with acid... Cartoons on TV have lots of pornography, such as Decoding DNV. Many students think it is a good show. They think it has good stuff such as romance and sex. Some students don't know cartoons have such stuff. Once they discover it, they will become interested too. Media has something to do with the recent increase of juvenile crime. I saw a report on TV. There is a street near Sichuan University. It is full of shops showing x-rated movies. It is inexpensive. Many middle-class students go there.

Another student agrees,

> TV and VCDs have a great influence on students. They imitate what they see on TV and VCDs such as fighting, robbery, bullying, and wearing strange clothes. For example, some students wear clothes with nails on it. Their clothing conveys the statement that they are untouchable. Newspapers are very influential too. The West China Daily tends to vividly portray murder and robbery. A classmate was robbed on his way home from school one evening. It was on a major street. The criminals were teenagers.

The above interview excerpts clearly reveal the negative influences of media on the students. The students are very concerned about the negative influences of media, especially TV, movies, and newspapers. Other studies have similar findings. According to a government-sponsored study, the current social and cultural life in China contains overwhelming negative factors, which have harmed school moral education. Since the late 1980s, many unhealthy publications have become available to the public. Some of them are against the leadership of the CCP, the socialist system, and Chinese history and culture. Some introduce western ideology, the capitalist worldview, and capitalist perspectives on politics, history, art, ethics, and values. Many video-audio products contain violence, sex and superstition (CCPCC and Central Institute for Educational Research 1990).

In conclusion, the conflicts between official teachings and social realities largely undermine the effectiveness of the moral education curriculum. The radical changes in national economic policies and the overwhelming power of media convey contradictory messages to the students that greatly contribute to students' skepticism toward the regime-sponsored values and ideology.

## Policy Vs Implementation

In ecological research, the properties of the person and of the environment, the structure of environmental settings, and the processes taking place within and between them must be viewed as interdependent and analyzed in systems terms. (Bronfenbrenner 1979:41)

In accordance with the interconnection principle of the ecological theory (Bronfenbrenner 1979), a student's moral learning is not an isolated process but the result of the interactions of environmental contexts at different levels. This study finds that the students' moral learning and development is impaired because their social environments of home, school, and society are at odds in terms of moral education. There is a lack of mutually positive feeling, goal consent, and supportive activities among the state, society, and the school.

It is believed that the conflicting goals at the state level and the school level are a major factor contributing to the problematic moral education at Central High School. The state intends to inculcate among the youth loyalty and support of the CCP and its socialism with Chinese Characteristics. But the school's primary concern is to raise test scores and attract publicity. Different goals result in different practices. Thus there is an obvious inconsistency between the state moral education policy and the school's implementation of this policy at Central High School.

To the state, moral education is a tool for achieving ideological conformity and ensuring social solidarity, which is believed to be essential for economic growth. As Bakken (2000) notes, China's reform program is a controlled-change program. The government never intends to lose its control over Chinese society. The government's open policy is intended to build a strong economy on which the CCP's legitimacy is based. Therefore, whenever the negative effects of the reform program are considered threatening to the regime, ideological campaigns are used to slow down the run-away engine of reform. This partially explains why the government has repeatedly issued directives urging strengthening moral education in the secondary schools as well as in elementary schools and universities.

In order to survive and prosper, the school can use the moral education curriculum as a tool to discipline the students to encourage better academic performance as well as garner publicity for the school. As discussed previously, the school sets as its primary goals improvements in test scores and increased prestige. The classification of students, evaluation measures for student conduct, and the competitive school environment all reveal the unofficial goals of the taught moral curriculum at Central High School.

Such conflicting goals result in the employment of different strategies and a hidden school agenda at Central High School. The obvious contradictions between the official rhetoric and school practices inevitably causes confusion and resentment among the students toward the taught moral curriculum.

In addition, it is a widely accepted notion that there is a lack of societal support for school moral education. As a result of the economic reform, Chinese society has become profit-driven. Although the government advocates that *deyu jidi* (moral education centers) be established off-campus with community support and resources in order to facilitate school moral education, the program has not been successful due to the lack of moneytary incentive.

For example, as one of the school officials points out, the military training at Central High School suffers from a lack of support from local military units. Military training used to be an intensive program of several weeks conducted at a military base. Students were required to reside on a military campus away from home for several weeks. The students lived with soldiers, ate at the military cafeteria, wore military uniforms, and participated in drilling and training exercises like target shooting. But now military units are no longer willing to cooperate with the school because there is little monetary reward involved. Therefore, the military training has been reduced to one-week of drilling on campus conducted by a couple of soldiers sent from the military base.

## Pragmatic Ideology

According to Bronfenbrenner, there is a striking phenomenon pertaining to settings at all three levels of the ecological environment.

Within any culture or subculture, settings of a given kind, such as homes, streets, or offices—tend to be very much alike, whereas between cultures they are distinctively different. It is as if within each society or subculture there existed a blueprint for the organization of every type of setting. Furthermore, the blueprint can be changed, with the result that the structure of the settings in a society can become markedly altered and produce corresponding changes in behavior and development. (1979:4)

It is believed that pragmatism is currently the overarching ideology that heavily influences Chinese secondary school moral education as well as other aspects of Chinese society. Deng innovated a rather pragmatic ideology to guide his reform program during its early stages (Goldman and MacFarquhar 1999; Goldman and Nathan 2000, White 1995). Deng believed that the ideology under Mao no longer a unifying creed and it is necessary to redefine the official ideology to create a basis for their new regime. Deng sees economic growth as the only way to increase the legitimacy of the party-state and he has replaced Mao's politics in command with economics in command. Deng altered Mao's ideological framework to meet the needs of market socialism. According to Goldman and Nathan (2000), some of his famous motifs are "It does not matter whether the cat is black or white, so long as it catches mice" (p. 310) representing fundamental pragmatism, "feeling for the stones while crossing the river" (p. 310) to illustrate the uncertainty of the path, and "to get rich is glorious" (p. 311) as a deliberate affirmation of individual prosperity.

Deng's pragmatic reform ideology, characterized by his cat analogy, has become prevalent in all aspects of Chinese society. It is believed that pragmatism has become the blueprint for Chinese society and is responsible for many problems including those in the arena of moral education.

The presence of pragmatism can be seen at all levels of the ecological scheme. At the policymaking level, the state is pragmatic in the way it utilizes moral education. The state considers moral education as a thought-control tool to offset negative influences in the reform process. China's reform is controlled change; that is, control is integrated into the reform program to prevent the engine of reform from running off track (Bakken 2000). The state has persistently stressed moral education since the beginning of the reform in the late 1980s. For example, special emphasis was placed on moral education to counter not only the spiritual pollution present during the period 1983–1984, but also the bourgeois liberation in 1987 and the peaceful evolution in the early 1990s (Lee 1996).

In addition, the current regime considers education to be a tool to build the labor force for the new economic order and therefore moral education has been modified to develop individuals with initiative, enterprise, self-respect and self-confidence as well as persons willing to take on risks and responsibilities. Some modern concepts such as the market, information and commodity, as well as the value of individuals, are discussed in the moral curriculum and official rhetoric. It is important to note that changes to moral education policy are intended to further the practical purposes of state building rather than for the interest of individuals.

At the local school level, the implementation of the intended moral curriculum also reflects a pragmatic ideology. The school officials are pragmatic in that they give priority to the survival and prosperity of the school over students' moral development. They cleverly make use of moral education to advance their own agenda. As discussed earlier, Central High School pragmatically utilized moral education measures to improve academic performance and school prestige. For example, although the quantification of students' conduct is widely believed both by teachers and students to be problematic, the school insists on using it because it is practical for management.

Moreover, driven by this pragmatic trend, the school is found to apply unprincipled or immoral methods in order to attain its goals. For example, in an interview a teacher mentions that, because the state allocation of resources is largely based on each school's academic record as determined by standardized exams, the teachers are given the hint to ignore the cheating behaviors of students during those exams.

The students have embraced pragmatism too. They openly pronounce that they are a generation of pragmatists. Their value systems and coping strategies clearly bear the influence of pragmatism. They tend to make moral judgments based on practical grounds rather than on moral principles.

For example, 56 percent of the questionnaire respondents believe that cheating on exams is wrong (see Table B-13, Appendix B), yet an analysis of students' written responses suggests that they believe cheating is wrong largely because it interferes with teaching and learning activities or because it causes a loss of face.

During the third week of the fall semester, students in one class were asked to reflect in their journal on a fellow student who stole a math test paper from the teacher's office. All the students pointed out that it was wrong for the student to cheat on the exam. However, in their writing the students seem to ignore the harm to his moral character; rather, they emphasized the consequences of his wrongdoing.

All the students strongly expressed their disgust and anger toward the cheater because he damaged the reputation of their class as well as interfered with the process of teaching and learning. They accused him of making their class look bad in front of other classes. As one student writes,

After class, we learned that he cheated on the exam. It is hard to believe that cheating happened in our class because it is the key-class of Senior Two. We all understand that it means teachers will be suspicious about our class and will doubt our test results. Teacher Chen (pseudonym) insisted that the test answers were stolen by students from other classes and given to our class. But our classmate soon admitted that he stole the test answers from the office. Thus, our title of the Most Excellent Class, which we worked so hard to gain, will become a laughing-stock among others who will say it is fake, totally superficial.

It is obvious that this student cares about the reputation of his class. There is no mention in his writing about cheating being morally wrong. The student shows great concern about his class losing face. Although students tend to put their own interest above the interest of the collective as discussed earlier, they are conscious about the reputation of their collective.

The study also finds that the students' responses not only reveal their concern for the reputation of their collective but also their pragmatic way of thinking. Pragmatism is obvious throughout their interview accounts and writing. As one student states,

I don't think it was worth it because this exam doesn't have a life-long impact on us. It is not as important as the final exam, even less important than the national university entrance examination. Cheating on this exam is meaningless. But he did it. As a result, this insignificant exam may become a stain on him all his life. It is like *touji bucheng daopei yibami* (a thief used up the bait but didn't get the chicken).

Clearly, this student is suggesting that if the exam was important and had a significant impact on his future, or if he would not be caught, cheating would be worth it. His comments again indicate that students render their judgment on moral issues from a pragmatic perspective. They do not pay much attention to the cheating itself; rather, they make moral judgments based on consequences. Face or sense of shame is also influential in their moral judgments. Students condemn cheating largely because it brings shame to the collective.

In conclusion, this study reveals that both the dynamics of the school setting and the social milieu in which it is imbedded have shaped the moral curriculum in Chinese secondary schools. Within the school setting, the lack of supportive environmental factors—mutual trust, positive feelings, a sense of common goals, and a balance of power—is found to be complicit in the development of the students' negative attitudes. Not only is the school context unfavorable for students' moral learning, the social, cultural and economic contexts beyond the school and their interconnections create difficulties in instilling the officially intended values and ideology at Central High School. The study finds that pragmatic ideology, Marxist philosophy, the culture of face, economic policy, popular values and media, as well as the conflicts between school teaching and social reality, all play an important role in shaping students' attitudes toward the moral education curriculum.

# 7

## CONCLUSION

Despite the implementation of numerous reform policies and much official rhetoric, moral education in China has failed to instill socialist morality among youth (Chan 1997). However, the major contributing factors for this failure are the subject of controversy among scholars, policymakers, administrators and teachers.

This study presents a student perspective on the problem of moral education in Chinese secondary schools. Taking a qualitative approach, this study utilizes participant observation and in-depth interviews as well as a student questionnaire to study the student's attitudes toward the moral education curriculum taught at Central High School.

This study finds that a majority of students at Central High School respond negatively toward the regime-sponsored values and ideology in the intended moral education curriculum, such as collectivism, socialism, communism, and the CCP. A majority of them despise self-sacrifice and put their own interest above the interest of the collective. They have many doubts about socialism with Chinese Characteristics and little faith in communist beliefs. They strongly object to the association between patriotism and the love of the CCP and its socialist ideology. It is evident that a majority of students at Central High School are indeed a pragmatic generation and indifferent to the regime-sponsored values and ideology in the intended moral education curriculum.

Moreover, this study finds that a majority of students at Central High School respond negatively to the implementation of the officially intended moral education curriculum at their school. They are dissatisfied with some of the moral education practices of the school, such as the campaign of learning from Lei Feng, student conduct evaluations, and the examination-oriented school culture. They believe that the campaign of learning from Lei Feng is reduced to a forced, superficial, and short-lived event of sweeping streets and bicycle cleaning at the school level and it carries the message of insincerity and hypocrisy. They also suggest that the scoring system of conduct evaluation is not cultivating moral character, but encouraging the wrong motives for good behaviors.

In addition, an overwhelming majority of students at Central High School do not believe teachers model the very regime-sponsored values that they are teaching. It is noteworthy that not only the so-called problem students in slow classes have complaints but also the well-adjusted students in advanced classes have negative attitudes toward their teachers.

It is obvious that the implementation of the moral education curriculum at Central High School does not help students internalize the regime-sponsored values and ideology. Moreover, this study reveals that students tend to take advantage of the current practices of moral education, especially its over-emphasis on outward performance, to achieve their personal aims, which oftentimes contradict the official values and ideology.

Guided by the ecological theory of human development (Bronfenbrenner 1979), this study finds multiple environmental factors contributing to the students' negative attitudes toward the moral education curriculum. Central High School fails to provide a favorable setting for students' moral learning in terms of activities, interpersonal relations and role expectations. Moral learning activities at Central High School lack variety, complexity and student initiation. There is little positive feeling between teachers and students and the latter have no sense of control over moral learning. In general, the school does not make moral character or conduct a primary expectation for its students while students' high expectations of teachers as role models contrast with teacher's problematic methods and conduct.

This study also finds that students' negative attitudes toward the moral education curriculum largely result from conflicts between the school and the more remote settings in the larger society. Official values and ideology prescribed in the intended moral curriculum contradict the social realities in the surrounding society. For example, the Chinese economic system is undergoing privatization while the school is still preaching socialism with Chinese Characteristics. Moreover, this study finds that media is a powerful agent that brings the outside world into the students' lives and exposes them to the social realities that largely contradict what they are taught at school.

Also, national economic changes, especially in relation to a parent's employment condition, have greatly influenced student's attitudes toward the moral education curriculum.

Based on the findings of this study, several observations can be made. Firstly, moral education is reduced from an end to a means at Central High School. Every party that is involved manipulates the moral education curriculum at Central High School. The school bends the officially intended moral curriculum to fit its own agenda. In order for the school to survive and prosper, the school's leadership utilizes the intended moral curriculum for the advancement of the school in terms of academics and reputation. Learning activities of the moral education curriculum as well as its management and administration are geared to achieve prestige for the school and better test scores.

Teachers at Central High School are selective in their enforcement of policies and requirements of the moral education curriculum. They focus on discipline and rules, which produce good behaviors and create a good learning environment. The rest of the moral education curriculum is largely ignored.

Moreover, students at Central High School manipulate the moral education curriculum for personal gain. They identify with the official teachings in examinations and fulfill official requirements while holding on to their own beliefs and moral framework. They make use of the official policies and requirements to achieve personal goals that oftentimes contradict what is intended in the formal moral education curriculum. Due to the focus on outward behaviors rather than internal character, students tend to act to fulfill the requirements rather than internalizing the moral teachings.

It is fair to say that, to some extent, moral education at Central High School becomes a show. Every party involved in the moral education curriculum at Central High School puts on the prescribed performance. Everybody follows the rule that they may attend to their unpronounced needs as long as they do not interfere with others. As Bakken (2000) suggests, Chinese society is an exemplary society and everybody puts on a show on the stage of the social theatre in which lying becomes a form of resistance to social conformity.

Secondly, the dilemmas of moral education at Central High School are reflections of the existing dilemmas at every level in Chinese society. The government, school administrators, teachers and students are all troubled at each level. At the state level, there is a tension between producing obedient citizens in order to maintain the social/political stability of the society, and cultivating creative and daring people for the needs of the growing economy. As China emerges into a modern society, young people are more free-spirited than their parent's generation. In the future it will be even more difficult to reconcile this contradiction and the dilemma can only become more severe.

A dilemma is also implicit in the regime-sponsored values and ideology as illustrated by the phrase socialism with Chinese Characteristics. The state-sponsored values and ideologies, especially the so-called socialism with Chinese Characteristics, are paradoxical. In order to maintain its rule over the country, the CCP tries to build its legitimacy on economic growth, yet the side effects of economic reform have unfavorable effects on the regime itself. As a result of the reform policy, the Chinese people are becoming more independent-minded and less committed to socialism and the CCP. They no longer believe in the superiority of socialism over capitalism and the necessity of the one-party political system. Ironically, the regime is undermined by its very efforts to strengthen its own legitimacy (White 1995).

Schools face the dilemma of how to maintain a good standing with the official requirements on moral education while striving to survive competition in the market economy. As the result of the market economy, schools in China have become more profit-driven. Schools have more financial responsibility as well as more autocracy under the principal-responsibility system. The state is only responsible for teachers' salaries and it is the principal's job to find money for other expenses. Therefore, while the state is concerned about social conformity and obedience to authority, schools are mainly concerned about attracting students and raising funds. Improvements in academic performance and school prestige become the de facto and sometimes obvious agenda for many Chinese schools.

Teachers are caught in a dilemma too. By tradition, they are considered role models of the students or examples of virtue. However, Chinese society has changed and the teachers are exposed to the influences of materialism, commercialism, consumerism and western ideas. There is a tension between the social expectations for teachers and teachers' personal conduct. Also, the teachers are caught between teaching the truth and preaching the untrue. It is not an easy task to cope with the conflicts between what the regime has sponsored and what they believe personally, especially for those who teach courses in the fields of politics, history or language arts. Oftentimes, these teachers have to compromise their uprightness and honesty. They might tell the students what they believe is right but advise the students to only give officially accepted answers in exams.

As for students, their lives are full of dilemmas. What is stated in textbooks and in the official rhetoric is different from what they observe in society. What the teachers and administrators say may differ from what they actually do. The students are forced to compete fiercely with each other while maintaining a spirit of collectivism. They are encouraged to be independent-minded and risk-taking, yet they are punished for these very qualities. They are under a heavy study load and are expected to voluntarily participate in activities of patriotic education and learning from Lei Feng. Moreover, they are taught insincerity and untruthfulness through the hidden curriculum while they are expected to be the very opposite. It is no wonder that many of them confess to being confused, bewildered, and distressed.

Thirdly, the importance of the role of the state in moral education at Central High School has largely decreased. Traditionally, the Chinese educational system has always been highly centralized. Under the communist regime, it was a highly unified system with a standardized administrative structure, curriculum and instruction, and evaluation measures. The central government exercised tight control over education, especially in the area of moral and ideological education.

However, this has begun to change. The government's control over moral education has loosened considerably in the past two decades. School administrators, teachers and students in Chinese secondary schools no longer passively accept moral education policy and practices. They are playing a much more important role in shaping the policymaking process and adapting those policies and regulations to fit their needs.

As a result of the reforms and other factors, politics—and political strategies—in much of China have become more local (Lieberthal 1995). Many local officials now regard national politics in Beijing as something to avoid. They feel that their careers will benefit most by protecting their supporters and by contributing to local prosperity and improvements in the standard of living. They only pay lip service to the slogans that are advanced by the state in order to lobby the state for resources. To some extent, school administrators and teachers are seen as policymakers because they alter the officially intended moral education curriculum to serve their own agendas, which has largely shaped what moral education is like in China today.

Students also play an active role in school moral education practice. They are not passive recipients of the moral education curriculum. Instead, they develop their own coping strategies, which allow them to make use of the official policies and requirements in order to achieve personal gains. They manipulate the system to attain their own goals, which oftentimes contradict what is intended in the formal moral education. For example, they are able to perform well and obtain a good conduct evaluation in the mathematical evaluation system without necessarily conforming to the officially desired values and ideology.

Despite the influence of the central authorities, Chinese local communities, families, and individuals play an active role in the transformation process engineered by the central government. The Chinese people often tacitly selected and exploited those elements in school system reform that they found useful, adjusting the intended content of some components and ignoring the rest (Thogerson 2001). This largely explains why the officially intended moral curriculum that may look promising on paper turns out to have unforeseen results.

Finally, whether moral education in Chinese secondary schools is a failure or not largely depends on how it is perceived. Many studies conducted by Chinese researchers as well as by Western researchers suggest that moral education in Chinese schools is rather problematic (Bakken 1991, 2000; Chan 1997; M. Li 1990; Z. Li 1997; Meyer 1990; Price 1992; Shao 1996; Thogerson 1990). It is true that moral education fails to transform the student's existing moral framework into the desired socialist moral framework (Chan 1997). However, for the schools that implement the officially intended moral curriculum, moral education has been a success in that it serves the agenda of the schools quite effectively.

Based on the findings of this study, some recommendations can be made. First of all, policymakers and administrators should be aware of the complexity of the issue of moral education and take a holistic approach to moral education reform. Obviously, moral education in Chinese secondary schools is not merely a methodological issue. It is tightly interwoven with politics as well as deeply rooted in the psychology of the Chinese people and Confucian philosophy. The recent trends in the field of Chinese moral education—the affective approach, the activities approach, or the systematic approach—each tackle a different aspect of moral education. A single simple approach will not be sufficient. A more holistic approach is needed to transform moral education in Chinese schools.

Secondly, the problem of treating moral education as a means instead of an end should be addressed. Once morality deviates from an end to being a means of serving other purposes, moral education becomes vulnerable to being deliberately manipulated and twisted. Traditionally, Chinese moral education has always been a tool of the ruling regime to maintain social conformity and obedience to authority. While retaining certain valuable elements from traditional moral learning strategies and methods, it is necessary to transform the political and cultural elements that hinder moral learning. Moral education should be person-centered rather than institution-centered.

Thirdly, the professional ethics of teachers and administrators involved in moral education should receive more attention. Teacher training and in-service evaluation should incorporate professional ethics as an important component. Consistency in moral education is crucial. Teachers and administrators should be aware that "Do what I say and not what I do" does not work in education, especially in the area of moral education. Teachers and administrators should be consistent in how they conduct themselves and in what they teach students.

In order to establish truly student-oriented education, it is important for teachers and administrators to have a constructive conception of students. They should view students as individuals at a formative age with great potential and unique developmental characteristics. Students should be considered growing persons rather than an asset or resource to serve their own agendas. Interaction with students in the classroom and beyond should be handled with special care. Teachers and administrators should treat students with honor and respect to build a healthy nurturer—learner relationship. It is especially important to increase mutual trust and positive feelings between teachers and students.

However, it is unfair that moral education workers at local schools sometimes are criticized for the ineffectiveness of moral education. It should be noted that some of the problems associated with moral education are inherent in the system and far beyond the workers' control, for example, the over-emphasis on test scores and the lack of enthusiasm for moral education. Policymakers should be more aware of the challenges these moral education workers face everyday. Their hard work, plights, and struggles should be taken into consideration in future reforms of moral education.

Finally, it is important to recognize that the interplay of elements and factors within the school setting and beyond is also crucial in moral education. The school environment and the diverse forces emanating from other settings in the larger society constantly interact with each other and create a dynamic context for student development. It is necessary to establish mutual trust and consented goals between teachers and parents and rally societal support from other social sectors to improve the effectiveness of school moral education.

In conclusion, it is important to note that some of the problems in the moral education curriculum as observed in this study are primarily ideological, social and cultural problems rather than curricula problems. As discussed earlier, the dilemmas of the moral education curriculum are largely a reflection of the dilemmas present in Chinese society. They will continue to trouble moral education at secondary schools as long as the dilemmas of Chinese society remain unresolved.

# APPENDIX A

## Students' Attitudes Questionnaire

Dear Student,

The following questionnaire is designed for my study on the moral education curriculum at your school. I would like to know what you really think about the moral education curriculum at your school. This questionnaire is not a test paper. There are no right or wrong answers to these questions. You don't need to give your name on the questionnaire. Please answer the questions true to yourselves. Thank you for your cooperation.

I. Please answer each question below by circling the correct answer(s).

1. Sex?
   (1) Male
   (2) Female

2. Grade?
   (1) Senior One
   (2) Senior Two
   (3) Senior Three

3. Age?
   (1) 14
   (2) 15
   (3) 16
   (4) 17
   (5) 18
   (6) 19
   (7) 20

4.  Only Child?
    (1) Yes
    (2) No

5.  Who do you live with?
    (1) Biological parents
    (2) Single parent
    (3) Remarried parent
    (4) Grandparents
    (5) Other _____

6.  Distance between home and school?
    (1) Within walking distance
    (2) 10 - 20 minutes ride by bike
    (3) 20 - 30 minutes ride by bike
    (4) more than 30 minutes ride by bike

7.  Father's occupation:
    (1) Factory worker
    (2) Clerk
    (3) *Fuwuyuan* (Waitor/Waitress)
    (4) *Yinyeyuan* (shopkeeper)
    (5) Doctor
    (6) Nurse
    (7) Engineer
    (8) Teacher
    (9) Scientist
    (10) Military Personnel
    (11) Wenti (Entertainer and Athlete)
    (12) Managers
    (13) Entrepreneur
    (14) Unemployed
    15) Getihu (Small business owner)
    (16) Other _____

8. Father's highest level of education:

    (1) Elementary or under
    (2) Junior high
    (3) Senior high or technical school
    (4) 3–year college
    (5) University or above
    (6) Other _____

9. Mother's occupation:
    (1) Factory worker
    (2) Clerk
    (3) *Fuwuyuan* (Waitor/Waitress)
    (4) *Yinyeyuan* (shopkeeper)
    (5) Doctor
    (6) Nurse
    (7) Engineer
    (8) Teacher
    (9) Scientist
    (10) Military Personnel
    (11)Wenti (Entertainer and Athlete)
    (12) Managers
    (13) Entrepreneur
    (14) Unemployed
    (15) Getihu (Small business owner*)*
    (16) Other _____

10. Mother's highest level of education:
    (1) Elementary or under
    (2) Junior high
    (3) Senior high or technical school
    (4) 3–year college
    (5) University or above
    (6) other _____

11. Were your parents ever considered as "Educated Youth" during the Cultural Revolution?
    (1) Father
    (2) Mother

12. Are your parents being laid-off?
    (1) Father
    (2) Mother

13. Is it likely that your parents will be laid-off?
    (1) Father
    (2) Mother

14. What are your parents' goals for your future career?
    (1) Factory worker
    (2) Clerk
    (3) Fuwuyuan (Waitor/Waitress)
    (4) Yinyeyuan (shopkeeper)
    (5) Doctor
    (6) Nurse
    (7) Engineer
    (8) Teacher
    (9) Scientist
    (10) Military Personnel
    (11) Wenti (Entertainer and Athlete)
    (12) Managers
    (13) Entrepreneur
    (14) Unemployed
    15) Getihu (Small business owner)
    (16) Other _____

15. What is your own career goal?
    (1) Factory worker
    (2) Clerk
    (3) Fuwuyuan (Waitor/Waitress)
    (4) Yinyeyuan (shopkeeper)
    (5) Doctor
    (6) Nurse
    (7) Engineer
    (8) Teacher
    (9) Scientist
    (10) Military Personnel
    (11) Wenti (Entertainer and Athlete)
    (12) Managers
    (13) Entrepreneur

(14) Unemployed

(15) Getihu (Small business owner)

(16) Other _____

16. What is the highest degree that your parents would like you to have?

    (1) Senior high

    (2) 3–year college

    (3) Universities

    (4) Master's

    (5) Doctorate

    (6) Other _____

17. What sort of relationship do you have with your father?

    (1) Ruler

    (2) Teacher

    (3) Friend

    (4) Stranger

    (5) Enemy

    (6) Other _____

18. What sort of relationship do you have with your mother?

    (1) Ruler

    (2) Teacher

    (3) Friend

    (4) Stranger

    (5) Enemy

    (6) Other _____

19. How many times do your parents come to school each semester?

    (1) Never

    (2) Once

    (3) 2 - 3 times

    (4) 4 times

20. How do your parents keep contact with your school?

    (1) Parents' meeting

    (2) Teacher's visit

    (3) Telephone

    (4) Contact

(5) Book
(6) Letter
(7) Notes
(8) School announcement
(9) Other _____

21. What about you do your parents pay most attention to?

(1) Health
(2) Studies
(3) Talents
(4) Character
(5) Skills
(6) Other _____

22. What do you talk about with your parents? (Select all that apply)
(1) Political issues
(2) Moral issues
(3) Family matters
(4) School happenings
(5) Your feelings/emotions
(6) Other _____

23. What is your total household income per month?
(1) $600 or under
(2) $600 - 1,000
(3) $1,000 - 3,000
(4) More than $3,000

24. Do your parents have difficulty paying your school fees?
(1) No problem at all
(2) Some problems
(3) Quite difficult
(4) Extremely difficult

25. What of the followings does your family have? (Select all that apply)
    (1) Computer
    (2) VCD
    (3) Sound system
    (4) TV
    (5) Telephone

26. Where do you usually get your information? (Select all that apply)
    (1) Internet
    (2) TV and Movies
    (3) Newspapers
    (4) Books
    (5) Magazines
    (6) Chatting with people
    (7) School
    (8) Other _____

27. What types of motives and TV programs do you prefer?
    (1) Action
    (2) Romance
    (3) Cartoon
    (4) Science fiction
    (5) News
    (6) Sports
    (7) "Focus"
    (8) "Sunshine"
    (9) "Animal World"
    (10) "Discovery"
    (11) Other _____

28. How much time do you spend watching TV/VCR/VCD each week?
    (1) Less than 10 hours
    (2) 10 - 15 hours
    (3) 16 - 20 hours
    (4) More than 20 hours
    (5) Other _____

29. What type of literature do you prefer?
    (1) Knight errant novels
    (2) World literary classics
    (3) Romantic novels
    (4) Revolutionary or war novels
    (5) Biographies
    (6) Other _____

30. What type of music do you prefer?
    (1) Folk music
    (2) Classical music
    (3) Western pop music
    (4) Cantonese and Taiwanese pop music
    (5) Mainland pop music

31. How do you spend your leisure time?
    (1) Shopping
    (2) Reading
    (3) Listening to music
    (4) Chatting
    (5) Sleeping
    (6) Watching TV
    (7) Playing computer games
    (8) Football
    (9) Tennis
    (10) Basketball
    (11) Dancing
    (12) Doing housework
    (13) other

32. What kind of student would those who really know you say you are?
    (1) Obedient
    (2) Naughty
    (3) Popular
    (4) Fashionable
    (5) Sporty
    (6) Confident
    (7) Skillful in leadership
    (8) Reserved

(9) Independent
(10) Ordinary
(11) Other

33. What sort of people do you like best as friends?
    (1) Excellent students
    (2) Loving, good towards others
    (3) Obvious strong points, wide interests
    (4) Clear of objectives to strive for, indomitable spirit
    (5) Some one who has lots of friends, who is good at personal relationships
    (6) Other _____

34. How many good friends do you in your class?
    (1) None
    (2) 1
    (3) 2–3
    (4) 4 or more

35. When you have problems, whom do you most depend on?
    (1) Teachers
    (2) Parents
    (3) Classmates
    (4) Friends
    (5) Other _____

36. Amongst high school students, what is the most trendy?
    (1) Going to colleges and universities
    (2) Famous name brands
    (3) Falling in love in high school years
    (4) Computer
    (5) Surfing the Net
    (6) Making friends
    (7) Chasing "stars"
    (8) Longing for home
    (9) Sports and exercises
    (10) Other _____

37. Which of the following activities do you get most out of?
    (1) Flag-raising ceremony
    (2) class meeting
    (3) Recreation and Sports activities
    (4) Watching a patriotic movie
    (5) Military training
    (6) Community welfare activities
    (7) Going to see an exhibition
    (8) Singing contest
    (9) Clean-up activities
    (10) Other _____

38. Which of the below methods most help your normal thinking?
    (1) Head teacher's work
    (2) Teachers' own example
    (3) Politics-ideology course
    (4) By relating to parents
    (5) Evaluation of student conduct
    (6) Social practice
    (7) Class and Youth League activities
    (8) Learning from models
    (9) Other _____

39. In the process of most students' growth and development, what do
    you consider to be the most important source of negative influence?
    (1) Family upbringing
    (2) Schooling
    (3) Interaction between students outside of school
    (4) General social mood
    (5) Popular media
    (6) Other _____

40. Who do you consider most embodies high moral character?
    (1) Scholars
    (2) Models
    (3) Political leaders
    (4) Friends
    (5) Father
    (6) Mother

(7) Head Teacher
(8) None
(9) Other _____

41. Who has most influenced your development as a person?
    (1) Parents
    (2) Teachers
    (3) Classmates
    (4) Friends
    (5) Communist Models
    (6) Sports stars
    (7) Pop stars
    (8) Movie stars
    (9) TV program presenter
    (10) Political leaders
    (11) Other _____

42. Who would do you consult when handling two thousand Yuan lost by other person?
    (1) Parents
    (2) Friends
    (3) Teacher
    (4) Yourself
    (5) Other _____

43. Which of the following moral character should be most promoted among students?
    (1) Sincerity and trustworthiness
    (2) Sense of responsibility
    (3) Courteous
    4) Tolerance
    (5) Integrity
    (6) Fair treatment of everyone
    (7) An enterprising spirit
    (8) Filial piety
    (9) Other _____

44. Among the following concepts, which do you esteem the highest?
    (1) Independence
    (2) Creativity

(3) Competitiveness
(4) Freedom
5) Democracy
(6) Rule of Law
(7) Openness
(8) Co-operation
(9) Environmental protection
(10) Tradition
(11) Pragmatism
(12) Other _____

45. Please list 10 persons whom you most admire (start with most important).

1. _____        6. _____

2. _____        7. _____

3. _____        8. _____

4. _____        9. _____

5. _____        10. _____

II. Please circle the appropriate letter using the following scale to indicate your agreement or disagreement with the following statements.

1    strongly disagree
2    moderately disagree
3    moderately neutral
4    neutral
5    strongly agree

1. Moral education is basically teaching the students to become a good person.

    1    2    3    4    5

2. Moral education is about morality and has little to do with ideology and politics.

   1   2   3   4   5

3. The main focus of moral education should be patriotism.

   1   2   3   4   5

4. The goals of the current school moral curriculum are Jiadakong (hypocritical, grandiose, and empty).

   1   2   3   4   5

5. The goals of the current moral curriculum are too idealistic for me.

   1   2   3   4   5

6. Highly moral people should have good morals and correct political thought.

   1   2   3   4   5

7. Moral education should include law, safety, sex and emotional character.

   1   2   3   4   5

8. Moral education is not closely enough related to daily life.

   1   2   3   4   5

9. I have found that all I have learned at school is applicable in daily life.

   1   2   3   4   5

10. The standard for high school student's daily behavior limits the development of their personality.

    1   2   3   4   5

11. Schooling overemphasizes political thought and overlooks morality and behavior training.

    1   2   3   4   5

12. Grades are more important than one's political stance.

    1   2   3   4   5

13. Moral education should penetrate every sector of the school's teaching and management.

    1   2   3   4   5

14. Modeling of teachers is the most effective way of conducting moral education.

    1   2   3   4   5

15. Most teachers are a good example for us.

    1   2   3   4   5

16. Language and history textbooks have too strong a political coloring.

    1   2   3   4   5

17. Most students have no interest in political studies.

    1   2   3   4   5

18. Teachers encourage me to have my own viewpoint about things.

    1   2   3   4   5

19. School should work closely with family and society.

    1  2  3  4  5

20. My parents have close contact with the school.

    1  2  3  4  5

21. My parents' viewpoint differs from what the school tries to instill.

    1  2  3  4  5

22. In the face of a wrong trend, the school's teachings appear pallid and weak.

    1  2  3  4  5

23. Exam-orientated schooling is not beneficial to students' moral thinking and development.

    1  2  3  4  5

24. My school has a good cultural, social and safety environment.

    1  2  3  4  5

25. I found my parents' teachings are more useful than what the school installs.

    1  2  3  4  5

26. My parents' understanding of and their feelings towards life have great influence on me.

    1  2  3  4  5

27. The society has greater influence on me than the school.

    1  2  3  4  5

28. My parents have bitterness and complaints toward life due to their experience.

    1   2   3   4   5

29. The vast majority of students agree that the value of human life is sacrifice.

    1   2   3   4   5

30. Patriotism is to love Socialism and the CCP.

    1   2   3   4   5

31. Communism will surely be realized in China.

    1   2   3   4   5

32. The vast majority of students will put the welfare of the collective above that of the individual.

    1   2   3   4   5

33. *Muomuowuwen* (work hard regardless of reward and recognition) is an important moral characteristic.

    1   2   3   4   5

34. The Youth League is not attractive to the vast majority of students any more.

    1   2   3   4   5

35. My ideal is to do what myself really want to do.

    1   2   3   4   5

36. The realization of one's ideal depends on one's own effort.

    1   2   3   4   5

37. When individual benefit conflicts with the nation's benefit, the vast majority of students would sacrifice their own benefit.

    1  2  3  4  5

38. When somebody in danger, the vast majority of students would volunteer to help.

    1  2  3  4  5

39. I wish I had more opportunities of participating social practice and extra curricular activities.

    1  2  3  4  5

40. The students in the 90s are a generation of pragmatism.

    1  2  3  4  5

41. Cheating in an exam is right when I am helping a friend.

    1  2  3  4  5

42. It is out of date to highly promote learning from Lei Feng in the 90s.

    1  2  3  4  5

# APPENDIX B

## Statistical Tables

### Table B-1: Number of Students by Grade and Class

| Grade | N | % | Class | N | % |
|---|---|---|---|---|---|
| Senior 1 | 147 | 38 | Advanced | 154 | 40 |
| Senior 2 | 47 | 38 | Average | 103 | 27 |
| Senior 3 | 92 | 24 | Slow | 129 | 33 |
| Total | 386 | 100 | Total | 386 | 100 |

### Table B-2: Parental Socio-Economic Statuses

| | | N | Total |
|---|---|---|---|
| Working Class[a] | Father | 232 | 60 |
| | Mother | 246 | 64 |
| Professional[b] | Father | 69 | 18 |
| | Mother | 42 | 11 |
| Other[c] | Father | 48 | 12 |
| | Mother | 67 | 17 |
| Unknown | Father | 37 | 10 |
| | Mother | 31 | 8 |
| Total | | 386 | 100 |

[a]Includes factory worker, clerk, waiter/waitress, shopkeeper.

[b]Includes doctor, nurse, engineer, teacher, scientist, manager, entrepreneur.

[c]Includes military personnel, entertainers, athletes, small business owners, and those without a regular job.

## Table B-3: Parental Employment Conditions

| Laid Off | | | | Expect Laying Off | | | | | |
|---|---|---|---|---|---|---|---|---|---|
| Father | | Mother | | Father | | Mother | | Total | |
| N | % | N | % | N | % | N | % | N | % |
| 42 | 11 | 56 | 15 | 33 | 9 | 38 | 10 | 386 | 100 |

## Table B-4: Student Families' Monthly Incomes

| ≤1000 *Yuan* | | 1000—3000 *Yuan* | | ≥3000 *Yuan* | | No Answer | | Total | |
|---|---|---|---|---|---|---|---|---|---|
| N | % | N | % | N | % | N | % | N | % |
| 177 | 46 | 175 | 45 | 3 | 6 | 11 | 3 | 386 | 100 |

## Table B-5: Student Responses to Collectivism

| The Vast Majority of Students Will Put the Welfare of the Collective above That of the Individual | | | | | | | |
|---|---|---|---|---|---|---|---|
| Disagree | | Agree | | Neutral | | Total | |
| N | % | N | % | N | % | N | % |
| 193 | 51 | 75 | 20 | 108 | 29 | 86 | 100 |

## Table B-6: Student Responses to Self-Sacrifice

| The Vast Majority of Students Agree That the Value of Human Life Is Self-Sacrifice | | | | | | | |
|---|---|---|---|---|---|---|---|
| Disagree | | Agree | | Neutral | | Total | |
| N | % | N | % | N | % | N | % |
| 188 | 49 | 65 | 17 | 128 | 34 | 386 | 100 |

## Table B-7: Student Responses to Patriotism

| Patriotism Is to Love Socialism and the CCP | | | | | | | |
|---|---|---|---|---|---|---|---|
| Disagree | | Agree | | Neutral | | Total | |
| N | % | N | % | N | % | N | % |
| 177 | 47 | 82 | 22 | 121 | 32 | 386 | 100 |

## Table B-8: Student Responses to Communism

| Communism Will Surely Be Realized in China | | | | | | | |
|---|---|---|---|---|---|---|---|
| Agree | | Disagree | | Neutral | | Total | |
| N | % | N | % | N | % | N | % |
| 108 | 29 | 118 | 31 | 153 | 40 | 386 | 100 |

## Table B-9: Student Responses to the Approach of Teachers as Role Models

| Modeling by Teachers Is the Most Effective Way to Conduct Moral Education | | | | | | | |
|---|---|---|---|---|---|---|---|
| Disagree | | Agree | | Neutral | | Total | |
| N | % | N | % | N | % | N | % |
| 32 | 9 | 255 | 68 | 91 | 24 | 386 | 100 |

## Table B-10: Student Responses to Teachers as Role Models

| Most Teachers Are Good Examples for Us | | | | | | | |
|---|---|---|---|---|---|---|---|
| Disagree | | Agree | | Neutral | | Total | |
| N | % | N | % | N | % | N | % |
| 157 | 41 | 107 | 28 | 118 | 31 | 386 | 100 |

## Table B-11: Student Rankings of People Embodying High Moral Character

| Ranking | People Embodying High Moral Character | N | % |
|---|---|---|---|
| 1 | Scholars | 330 | 86 |
| 2 | Communist Models | 127 | 33 |
| 3 | My Father | 97 | 25 |
| 4 | My Mother | 94 | 24 |
| 5 | National Leaders | 75 | 20 |
| 6 | Nobody | 56 | 15 |
| 7 | My Friend | 46 | 12 |
| 8 | My Head Master | 37 | 10 |
| 9 | No Answer | 9 | 2 |
| | Total | 386 | 100 |

## Table B-12: Student Channels of Information

| Ranking | Channels | N | % |
|---|---|---|---|
| 1 | TV or Movies | 336 | 87 |
| 2 | Newspapers | 334 | 87 |
| 3 | Chats with People | 232 | 60 |
| 4 | Magazines | 219 | 57 |
| 5 | Books | 204 | 53 |
| 6 | Teachers | 152 | 39 |
| 7 | Internet | 9 | 2 |
|  | Total | 386 | 100 |

## Table B-13: Student Responses to Cheating

| Cheating on an Exam Is Right When I Am Helping a Friend | | | | | | | |
|---|---|---|---|---|---|---|---|
| Disagree | | Agree | | Neutral | | Total | |
| N | % | N | % | N | % | N | % |
| 214 | 56 | 42 | 11 | 125 | 33 | 386 | 100 |

# BIBLIOGRAPHY

Bai, Limin. Monetary Reward Versus the National Ideological Agenda: Career Choice Among Chinese University Students. Journal of Moral Education 27(4):525–540.

Bakken, Borge. 1991 Modernizing Morality? Paradoxes of Socialization in China during the 1980s. East Asian History 1991–1992(2):125–141. 2000 The Exemplary Society: Human Improvement, Social Control, and the Dangers of Modernity in China. Oxford, England: Oxford University Press.

Ban, Hua. 1999 Jinshinianlai Deyu Sixiang Xiandaihua De Jinzhan (The Progress of Modernizing Moral Education Theory in the Past Decade). Jiaoyu Yanjiu (Educational Research) Febrary 1999:18–22. 2001 Chuangzaoxing De Peiyang Yu Xiandai Deyu (Cultivating Creativity and Moral Education in Contemporary Times). Jiaoyu Yanjiu (Educational Research) January 2001:15–19.

Ban, Hua and Zhengyong Wang. 1997 Gaozhong Banzhuren (The Senior Secondary School Class Master). Nanjing, China: Nanjing Shifan Daxue Chubanshe.

Bandura, Albert. 1977 Social Learning Theory. Englewood Cliffs, NJ: Prentice-Hall.

Bandura, Albert and H. Walters.1963 Social Learning and Personality Development. New York: Holt, Rinehart and Winston.

Bond, Michael Harris, ed.1986 The Psychology of the Chinese People. Hong Kong: Oxford University Press.

Bronfenbrenner, Urie. The Ecology of Human Development: Experiments by Nature and Design. Cambridge, MA: Harvard University Press.

Bronfenbrenner, Urie, et al. 1999 The State of Americans: This Generation and the Next. New York: Free.

Chan, Merry Jean. 1997 Performing Well in School: Situational Poetics and Moral Education in a Shanghai Junior Middle School. B.A. dissertation. Harvard University.

Chen, Kai-ming. 1995 Education—Decentralization and the Market. In Social Change and Social Policy in Contemporary China. Linda Wong and Stewart Macpherson, eds. p.70–87. Aldershot, England: Avebury.

Chen, Zhili, ed. 1999 Deng Xiaoping Lilun Zhidao Xiao De Zhongguo Jiaoyu Ershi Nian (Chinese Education in the Two Decades of Reform under the Guidance of Deng Xiaoping's Theory). Fuzhou, China: Fujian Jiaoyu Chubanshe.

Chin, Ann-ping. 1988 Children of China: Voices from Recent Years. New York: Knopf.

Chinese Communist Party Central Committee. 1989 Zhonggong Zhongyang Guanyu Gaige He Jiaoqiang Zhongxiaoxue Deyu Gongzuo De Tongzhi (A Notice Issued by the CCPCC Regarding the Reformation and Strengthening of Moral Education Work in Elementary and Secondary Schools). Renmin Ribao (People's Daily) January 17, 1989:1. 1994 Zhonggong Zhongyang Guanyu Jinyibu Jiaoqiang He Gaijin Xuexiao Deyu Gongzuo De Ruogan Yijian (Suggestions of the CCPCC on Further Strengthening and Improving School Moral Education Work). Renmin Ribao (People's Daily) September 9, 1994:1.

Chinese Communist Party Central Committee and Central Institute for Educational Research. 1990 She Hui Wen Hua Sheng Huo Yu Zhong Xue De Yu Diao Cha Wen Ji (Social and Cultural Life and Moral Education in Secondary Schools). Beijing, China: Zhongguo Renmin Daxue Chubanshe.

Chinese Communist Party Central Committee and State Council. 1993 Zhonguo Jiaoyu Gaige He Fazhan Gangyao (The Guideline for Educational Reform and Development in China). Renmin Ribao (People's Daily) February 27,1993:1. 2001 Zhonggong Zhongyang Bangongting Guowuyuan Bangongting Guanyu Shiying Xinxingshi Jinyibu Jiaoqiang He Gaijin Zhongxiaoxue Deyu Gongzu De Yijian (Suggestions of the Executive Office of the CCPCC and the Executive Office of State Council on Further Strengthening and Improving Moral Education Work in Elementary and Secondary Schools under New Situation). Renmin Ribao (People's Daily) January 18, 2001:1.

Cook, Thomas D. and Donald T. Campbell. 1979 Quasi-Experimentation: Design and Analysis Issues for Field Settings. Boston, MA: Houghton Mifflin.

Creswell, John W. 2002 Educational Research: Planning, Conducting, and Evaluating Quantitative and Qualitative Research. Upper Saddle River, NJ: Merrill Prentice.

Cuban, Larry. 1992 Curriculum Stability and Change. *In* Handbook of Research on Curriculum: A Project of the American Educational Research Association. Philip W. Jackson, ed. p. 216–247. New York: Macmillan.

Deng, Xiaoping. 1990 Zuijin Shiyian Zuida De Shibai Shi Zai Jiaoyu Fangmian (The Biggest Failure in the Past Decade Is Education). *In* Zhongguo Sixiang ZhengZhi Gongzuo Quanshu (A Compendium of Materials on Ideological and Political Work in China). Chuanhua Liu, Chen Lu and Bingjie Liu, eds. p. 528. Beijing, China: Renmin Daxue Chubanshe. 1994 Selected Works of Deng Xiaoping, 1982–1992. Bejing, China: Foreign Languages.

Denzin, Norman K. and Yvonna S. Lincoln. 1994 Strategies of Inquiry. *In* Handbook of Qualitative Research. N. K. Denzin and Y. S. Lincoln, eds. p.199–208. Thousand Oaks, CA: Sage.

Durkheim, Emile. 1973 Moral Education: A Study in the Theory and Application of the Sociology of Education. New York: Free.

Eisner, Elliot W. The Educational Imagination. New York: Macmillan. 1992 Curriculum Ideology. *In* Handbook of Research on Curriculum: A Project of the American Educational Research Association. Philip W. Jackson, ed. p. 302–326. New York: Macmillan.

Elder, Glen H. 1975 Adolescence in the Life Circle: An Introduction. *In* Adolescence in the Life Cycle: Psychological Change and Social Context. Sigmund E. Dragastin and Glen H. Elder eds. p.1–22. New York: Wiley.

Epstein, Epstein, Irving, ed. 1991 Chinese Education: Problems, Politics and Prospects. New York: Garland.

Fewsmith, Joseph. 1999 Elite Politics. *In* The Paradox of China's Post-Mao Reforms. Merle Goldman and Roderick MacFarquhar, eds. p. 47–75. Cambridge, MA: Harvard University Press.

Figurski, Thomas J. 2000 Moral Development. *In* Encyclopedia of Sociology. Vol.3. Edgar F. Borgatta and Rhonda J.V. Montgomery, eds. p.1894–1906. 2nd. ed. New York: Macmillan.

Firestone, W. A. 1987 Meaning in Method: The Rhetoric of Quantitative and Qualitative Research. Educational Researcher 16(7):16–21.

Gilligan, Carol. 1982 In a Different Voice: Psychological Theory and Women's Development. Cambridge, MA: Harvard University Press.

Goldman, Merle and Andrew J. Nathan. 2000 Searching for the Appropriate Model for the People's Republic of China. *In* Historical Perspectives on Contemporary East Asia. Merle Goldman and Andrew Gordon, eds. p. 297–320. Cambridge, MA: Harvard University Press.

Goldman, Merle and Roderick MacFarquhar, eds. The Paradox of China's Post-Mao Reforms. Cambridge, MA: Harvard University Press.

Goodlad, John. 1984 A Place Called School. New York: McGraw Hill.

Guba, Egon G. and Yvonna S. Lincoln. 1981 Effective Evaluation: Improving the Usefulness of Evaluation Results through Responsive and Naturalistic Approaches. San Francisco: Jossey-Bass. 1982 Epistemological and Methodological Bases of Naturalistic Inquiry. Educational Communication and Technology Journal 30(4): 233–252. 1989 Fourth Generation Evaluation. Newbury Park, CA: Sage.

Hawkins, John N. 1983 Education and Social Change in the People's Republic of China. New York: Praeger.

Howe, Kenneth R. Two Dogmas of Educational Research. Educational Researcher 14(8):10–18. 1988 Against the Quantitative-Qualitative Incompatibility Thesis or Dogmas Die Hard. Educational Researcher 17(8):10–16.

Hu, Dingnan. 1998 Zhongxiaoxue Deyu Gongzuo Jizhi (Institution of Moral Education Work in Secondary and Elementary Schools). *In* Xuexiao Deyu Gongzuo Quanshu (A Compendium of Materials on School Moral Education Work). Changmei Gao, ed. p. 432–441. Beijing, China: Jiuzhou Tushu Chubanshe.

Hu, Lizhen, Yihong Shia, and Hailing Sun. 1988 Dangdai Dazhongxuesheng De Sixiang Yu Xinli Tansuo (Exploring the Ideological and Psychological Conditions of the Contemporary College and Secondary Students). Renmin Daxue Baokan Fuying Ziliao *Ziliao* (People's University Copied Newspaper and Journal Materials) May 1988: 29–39.

Huo, Liyan. 2001 Jiaoyu De Zhuanxing Yu Jiaoshi Juese De Zhuanhuan (Transition of Educational Mode and Change of Teacher's Role in Education). Jiaoyu Yanjiu (Educational Research) March 2001:70.

Jackson, Philip W. 1968 Life in Classrooms. New York: Teachers College Press. Untaught Lessons. New York: Teachers College Press.

Jenkins, Susan K. 1992 Early Adolescent Values in Taiwan and Mainland China: An Exploratory Study. Ph.D. dissertation. University of Washington.

Jiang, Zemin. 1990 Carry On and Promote Patriotic Tradition in the New Historical Period. *In* Yuwen (Language and Literature). Renmin Jiaoyu Chubanshe Yuwen Ershi, ed. p.112–117. Shichuan, China: Renmin Jiaoyu Chubanshe.

Jiao, Shulan, et al. 1986 Comparative Study of Behavior Qualities of Only Children and Sibling Children. Child Development 57(2):357–361.

Jiao, Shulan, et al. 1986 Comparative Study of Behavior Qualities of Only Children and Sibling Children. Child Development 57(2):357–361.

Kohlberg, Lawrence. 1969 Stage and Sequence: The Cognitive-Development Approach to Socialization. *In* Handbook of Socialization Theory and Research. David Goslin, ed. p. 347–480. Chicago: Rand McNally.

———. 1971 From Is to Ought: How to Commit the Naturalist Fallacy and Get Away with It in the Study of Moral Development. *In* Cognitive Development and Epistemology. Theodore Mischel, ed. p.151–236. New York: Academic.

———. 1976 Moral Stages and Moralization: The Cognitive Developmental Approach. *In* Moral Development and Behavior: Theory, Research, and Social Issues. Thomas Lickona, ed. p. 31–53. New York: Holt, Rinehard, and Winston.

———. 1981 The Philosophy of Moral Development: Moral Stages and the Idea of Justice. San Francisco: Harper and Row.

———. 1984 The Psychology of Moral Development: the Nature and Validity of Moral Stages. San Francisco: Harper and Row.

Ku, Yu-chun. 1993 Moral Education in Taiwan Reconceptualization: The Problems of Adopting Western Models in an Era of Ecological Crisis. Ph.D. dissertation. University of Oregon.

Kwong, Julia. 1985 Changing Political Culture and Changing Curriculum: An Analysis of Language Textbooks in the People's Republic of China. Comparative Education 21(2):197–208.

———. 1994 Ideology Crisis among China's Youth: Values and Official Ideology. British Journal of Sociology 45(2):247–264.

Lai, Winnie Y. W. Auyeung. 1991 Curriculum Dissemination in the People's Republic of China. *In* Curriculum Development in East China. Colin Marsh and Paul Morris, eds. p. 82–105. London: Falmer.

Lamonstragne, Jacques. 1986 Educational Development in the P.R.C.: Regional and Ethnic Disparities. Issues and Studies 22(9):73–94.Educational Disparities in Mainland China: Characteristics and Trends. *In* Education in Mainland China: Review and Evaluation. Bin-Jaw Lin and Li-Min Fan, eds. p.130–152. Taipei, Taiwan: National Chenghua University.

Lamonstragne, Jacques and Ma, Rong. 1995 The Development of Education in China's Cities and Counties. *In* Social Change and Educational Development: Mainland China, Taiwan, and Hong Kong. G. A. Postiglione and W. O. Lee, eds. p. 153–173. Hong Kong: Center for Asian Studies Press.

Lee, Wing On. 1996 Guest Editor's Introduction. Chinese Education and Society 29(4):5–12.

Li, Chunsheng, et al. 1997 Shanghai Gaozhong Xuesheng Sixiang Zhuangkuang Diaocha Baogao (An Investigative Report on the Ideological Situation of Senior Secondary Students in Shanghai). Jiaoyu Yanjiu (Educational Research) May 1997:36–42.

Li, Gui, et al. 1989 An Investigative Survey of Conditions among Middle School Ideological and Political Workers in Beijing. Chinese Education 22(3):90–111.

Li, Guolin. 1988 Importance of Updating Educational Thinking as Seen from the Problem of Junior High School Dropouts in Guangzhou City Districts. Chinese Education 21(3):80–87.

Li, Maosen. 1990 Moral Education in the P.R.C. Journal of Moral Education 19(3):159–171.

Li, Shaojun. 1989 The Wave of Individualism. Chinese Education 23(1):92–112.

Li, Xueming. 1989 New Hot Issues for China's University Students. Chinese Education 23(1):83–86.

Li, Yanjie. 1990 Youth Educators Encounter a Challenge from the Young People: A Frank Dialogue between the Young People of Shekou and Qu Xiao and Li Yanjie. Chinese Education 23(1):48–49.

Li, Zhengang. 1997 Dangdai Zhangguo Daode Kunjing Yu Chulu (Moral Dilemma and Its Solutions in Modern China). Zhongguo Renmin Daxue Xuebao (Journal of People's University of China) January 1997:32–94.

Li, Zhixiang, et al. 1989 The Current Conditions of Those Involved in Ideological and Political Education of College and University Students: A Proposal. Chinese Education 22(3):9–33.

Lieberthal, Kenneth. 1995 Governing China: From Revolution through Reform. New York: W.W. Norton.

Lin, Changhua. 1998 Zhongxiaoxue Deyu Kaohe Lianghua (Quantification of Evaluation of Deyu in Elementary and Secondary Schools). *In* Xuexiao Deyu Gongzuo Quanshu (A Compendium of Materials on School Moral Education Work). Liu Bing, ed. p. 432–441. Beijing, China: Jiuzhou Tushu Chubanshe.

Lin, Huey Ya. 1988 A Confucian Theory of Human Development. *In* Oriental Theories of Human Development: Scriptural and Popular Beliefs from Hinduism, Buddhism, Confucianism, Shinto, and Islam. Thomas R. Murry, ed. p.117–133. New York: P. Lang.

Lin, Jing. 1993 Education in Post-Mao China. New York: Praeger.
———. 1994 The Opening of the Chinese Mind. New York: Praeger.
Link, Perry. 1994 China's "Core" Problem. *In* China in Transformation. Wei-ming Tu, ed. p. 189–205. Cambridge, MA: Harvard University Press.
Liu, Huiling. 1994 On Psychology of Moral Personality. Guangzhou, China: Guangdong Renmin Chubanshe.
Lo, Nai-Kwai L. 1986 Mao Zedong's Developmental Theories and Their Influence on Contemporary Chinese Education. Educational Journal 15(2):26–38.
Lo, Rita C. C. 2001 The Role of Class Teachers in a Key Secondary School in Shanghai. Pastoral Care March 2001:20–27.
Lu, Jie. 1995 Zaiyi Deyu zhi Xiangyong Gongneng (Rethinking of Moral Education's Enjoyment Function). Jiaoyu Yanjiu (Educational Research) June 1995:27–31.
———. 1999a Ren Dui Ren de Lijie: Daode Jiaoyu de Jichu (Mutual Understanding among Human Beings: The Basis of Moral Education). Jiaoyu Yanjiu (Educational Research) July 1999:3–54.
———. 1999b Zouxiang Shijie Lishi de Ren (On the Transformation and Education of Human Beings). Jiaoyu Yanjiu (Educational Research) November 1999:3–15.
Lu, Shu-Ping. 1990 The Development of Self-Conceptions from Childhood to Adolescence in China. Child Study Journal 20(2):129–137.
Lu, Youshuan. 1996 Zhongguo Gaige Kaifang Xingshi Xia Jiazhiguan De Chongtu yu Daode Jiaoyu (Value Conflicts and Moral Education under Reform and Open Policy in China). *In* Daode Yu Gongmin Jiaoyu (Morality and Citizenship Education). Guoqiang Liu and Ruiquan Li, eds. p. 199–214. Hong Kong: Hong Kong Institute of Educational Research.
Ma, Hing Keung. 1988 The Chinese Perspective on Moral Judgment Development. International Journal of Psychology 23(2):201–227.
MacFarquhar, Roderick. 1999 Dynamic Economy, Declining Party-State. *In* The Paradox of China's Post-Mao Reforms. Merle Goldman and Roderick MacFarquhar, eds. p. 1–27. Cambridge, MA: Harvard University Press.
Mao, Zedong. 1971 Selected Readings from Works of Mao Tsetung. Peking, China: Foreign Languages Press.
Maxwell, Joseph A. 1992 Understanding and Validity in Qualitative Research. Harvard Educational Review 62(3):279–300.
Mertens, Donna M. 1998 Research Methods in Education and Psychology: Integrating Diversity with Quantitative and Qualitative Approaches. Thousand Oaks, CA: Sage.
Meyer, Jeffery F. 1990 Moral Education in the People's Republic of China. Moral Education Forum 15(2):3–26.
Miles, Matthew B. and Michael A. Huberman. 1994 Qualitative Data Analysis: An Expanded Sourcebook. Thousand Oaks, CA: Sage.

Mok, Ka-ho. 2002 Marketization and Decentralization: Development of Education and Paradigm Shift in Social Policy. Hong Kong Public Administration 5(1):35–56.

Nunner-Winkler, G. 1993 Moral Development. *In* The International Encyclopedia of Education. Husén Torsten and T. Neville Postlethwaite, eds. p.3915–3920. Oxford, England: Pergamon.

Ogden, Suzanne. 2002 Global Studies. 9th ed. Gulford, CT: McGraw-Hill.

Paine, Lynn. 1986a In Search of a Metaphor to Understand China's Changes. Social Education 50(2):106–109.

———. 1986b Timeline of Chinese Policy Changes: 1949–1985. Social Education 50(2):110–111.

———. 1990 The Teacher as Virtuoso: A Chinese Model for Teaching. Teachers College Record 92(1):44–81.

Perlmutter, Rosanne and Ester R. Shapiro. 1987 Morals and Values in Adolescence. *In* Handbook of Adolescent Psychology. Vincent Van Hasselt and Michael Hersen, eds. p. 184–204. New York: Pergamon.

Piaget, Jean. 1932 The Moral Development of the Child. London: Kegan Paul.

Pollack, Jordan Ian. 1997 Civilizing Chinese: Efforts in Spiritual Construction at Shengzhen University. Ph.D. dissertation. University of Michigan.

Postiglione, Gerard A. and Wing On Lee, eds. 1995 Social Change and Educational Development: Mainland China, Taiwan and Hong Kong. Hong Kong: Center of Asian Studies Press.

Price, Ronald F. 1992 Moral-Political Education and Modernization. *In* Education and Modernization: The Chinese Experience. Ruth Hayheo, ed. p. 211–238. New York: Pergamon.

Pye, Lucian W. 1986 On Chinese Pragmatism in the 1980s. China Quarterly 106(6):207–234.

Qi, Wanxue. 1995 Chongtu Yu Zhenghe (Conflict and Integration). Jinan, China: Shandong Jiaoyu Chubanshe.

———. 1999 Huodong Daode Jiaoyu Muoshi De Lilun Gouxiang (Theoretical Structure and Practical Experiment of Activity-Based Moral Education Model). Jiaoyu Yanjiu (Educational Research) June 1999:69–76.

Raymond, Boudon. 1989 The Analysis of Ideology. Malcolm Slater, transl. Cambridge, England: Polity. (Original: L'idéologie, ou l'origine des idées reçues, Paris, 1986.)

Reed, Gay Garland. 1991 The Lei Feng Phenomenon in the People's Republic of China. Ph.D. dissertation. University of Virginia.

———. 1995a Looking in the Chinese Mirror: Reflections on Moral-Political Education in the United States. Educational Policy 9(3):244–259.

———. 1995b Moral/Political Education in the P.R.C.: Learning through Role Models. Journal of Moral Education 24(2):99–111.

Reichardt, Chales and Thomas Cook. 1979 Beyond Qualitative versus Quantitative Methods. *In* Qualitative and Quantitative Methods in Evaluation Research.

Thomas D. Cook and Charles S. Reichardt, eds. p. 7–32. Beverly Hills, CA: Sage.

Reymond, Williams. 1985 Keywords: A Vocabulary of Culture and Society. New York: Oxford University Press.

Rosen, Stanley. 1989 Value Changes among Post-Mao Youth: The Evidence from Survey Data. *In* Unofficial China: Popular Culture and Thought in the People's Republic of China. Perry Link, Richard Madsen and Paul G. Pickowicz, eds. p. 193–216. Boulder, CO: Westview.

———. 1990a The Impact of Reform on the Attitudes and Behavior of Chinese Youth: Some Evidence from Survey Research. *In* Political Implications of Economic Reform in Communist Systems. Donna L. Bahry and Joel C. Mosess, eds. p. 262–293. New York: New York University Press.

———. 1990b The Impact of Reform Policies on Youth Attitudes. *In* Chinese Society on the Eve of Tiananmen: The Impact of Reform. Deborah Davis and Ezra F. Vogel, eds. p. 283–305. Cambridge, MA: Harvard University Press.

———. 1991 Political Education. *In* Chinese Education: Problems, Politics and Prospects. Irving Epstein, ed. p. 416–449. New York: Garland.

———. 1992 New Directions in Secondary Education. *In* Education and Modernization: The Chinese Experience. Ruth Hayheo, ed. p. 65–92. New York: Pergamon.

———. 1994 Chinese Students in the Nineties Adjusting to the Market. China News Analysis August 1–15,1994:1–12.

Rosenbaum, Arther Lewis, ed. 1992 State and Society in China: The Consequences of Reform. Boulder, CO: Westview.

Ross, Heidi. 1991 "Crisis" in Chinese Secondary Schooling. *In* Chinese Education: Problems, Politics and Prospects. Irving Epstein, ed. p. 66–108. New York: Garland.

———. 1993 China Learns English: Language Teaching and Social Change in the People's Republic of China. New Haven, CT: Yale University Press.

Rossman, G.B. and B. L. Wilson. 1990 Numbers and Words Revisited: Being "Shamelessly Eclectic." Evaluation Review 9(5):627–643.

Sautman, Barry. 1991 Politicization, Hyperpoliticization, and Depoliticization of Chinese Education. Comparative Education Review 35(4):670–689.

Schoenhals, Martin. 1993 The Paradox of Power in a People's Republic of China Middle School. Armonk, NY: Sharpe.

Schofield, Janet W. 1990 Increasing the Generalizability of Qualitative Research. *In* Qualitative Inquiry in Education. E. Eisner and A. Peshkin, eds. p.201–232. New York: Teachers College Press.

State Education Commission. 1998a Guojia Jiaowei Guanyu Banfa Zhongxiaoxue Deyu Gongzu Guichen (A Notice of the SEC on Issuing Operational Regulations for Moral Education Work in Elementary and Secondary Schools). Internal Circulation of the SEC. Retrieved Feburary 15, 2003 from http//:www.moe.gov.cn

―――. 1998b Guojia Jiaowei Guanyu Zhengshi Banfa Zhongxue Deyu Dagang De Tongzhi (A Notice of the SEC on Issuing the Guideline for Secondary School Moral Education). *In* Xuexiao Deyu Gongzuo Quanshu (A Compendium of Materials on School Moral Education Work). Gao Changmei, ed. p. 561–572. Beijing, China: Jiuzhou Tushu Chubanshe.

―――. 1998c Jiaoyubu Guanyu Banfa Xiaoxuesheng Richang Xingwei Guifan De Tongzhi (A Notice of the Ministry of Education on Issuing Everyday Behavior Standards for Elementary School Students). *In* Xuexiao Deyu Gongzuo Quanshu (A Compendium of Materials on School Moral Education Work). Gao Changmei, ed. p. 585–587. Beijing, China: Jiuzhou Tushu Chubanshe.

―――. 1998d Jiaoyubu Guanyu Banfa Zhongxuesheng Richang Xingwei Guifan De Tongzhi (A Notice of the Ministry of Education on Issuing Everyday Behavior Standards for Secondary School Students). *In* Xuexiao Deyu Gongzuo Quanshu (A Compendium of Materials on School Moral Education Work). Gao Changmei, ed. p.581–585. Beijing, China: Jiuzhou Tushu Chubanshe.

―――. 1998e Jiaoyubu Guanyu Banfa Zhongxuesheng Shouze He Xiaoxuesheng Shouze De Tongzhi (A Notice of the Ministry of Education on Issuing Regulations for Secondary School Students and Elementary School Students). *In* Xuexiao Deyu Gongzuo Quanshu (A Compendium of Materials on School Moral Education Work). Gao Changmei, ed. p. 588–589. Beijing, China: Jiuzhou Tushu Chubanshe.

Shanahan, James and Michael Morgan. 1992 Adolescents, Families and Television in Five Countries. Journal of Educational Television 18(1):33–35.

Shao, Daosheng. 1996 Zhongguo Shehui De Kunjin (The Plight of Chinese Society). Beijing, China: Shehui Kexue Wenxue Chubanshe.

Shirk, Susan. 1982 Competitive Comrades: Career Incentives and Student Strategies in China. Berkeley, CA: University of California Press.

Sieber, Sam D. 1973 The Integration of Field Work and Survey Methods. American Journal of Sociology 78(6):1335–1359.

Simpson, Elizabeth L. 1974 Moral Development Research: A Case Study of Scientific Cultural Bias. Human Development 17(2):81–106.

Smith, P. K, Helen Cowie, and Mark Blades. 1998 Understanding Children's Development. 3rd ed. Oxford, England: Blackwell.

Snarey, John. 1997 Cross-cultural Universality of Social-Moral Development: A Critical Review of Kohlbergian Research. Psychological Bulletin 97(2): 202–232.

―――. 1992 Moral Education. *In* Encyclopedia of Educational Research, Vol. 3. 6th ed. Marvin C. Alkin, Michele Linden, Jana Noel, and Karen Ray, eds. p. 856–860. New York: Macmillan.

Stake, Robert E. 1994 Case Studies. *In* Handbook of Qualitative Research. N. K. Denzin and Y. S. Lincoln, eds. p. 236–247. Thousand Oaks, CA: Sage.

―――. 1995 The Art of Case Study Research. Thousand Oaks, CA: Sage.

Su, Songxin. 1998 Cong Chuantong Xiang Ziwuo Xiang Taren Jiazhi Daoxiang De Zhuanbian (From Tradition to Orientation toward Self and Others). Dangdai Qingnian Yanjou (Research on Youth) April 1998:1–5.

Sun, Xiting, et al. 1995 Ren de Zhutixing Neihan yu Ren de Zhutixing Jiaoyu (On Human Nature and Human Oriented Education). Jiaoyu Yanjiu (Educational Research) October 1995:34–39.

Tao, Wuxian and Rongxuan Wang, eds. 1999 Chengdu Wushinian (Fifty Years of Chengdu). Beijing, China: Zhongguo Tongji Chubanshe.

Teng, Teng. 1988 Zhongxiaoxue Deyu Shi Shehui Jingshen Wenming Jianshe De Dunji Gongcheng (Elementary and Middle School Moral Education, the Very Foundation of Society's Spiritual Civilization). Renmin Jiaoyu (People's Education) September 1988:2.

Thogerson, Stig. 1990 Secondary Education in China after Mao: Reform and Social Conflict. Aarhus, Denmark: Aarhus University Press.

———. 2001 State and Society in Chinese Education. *In* Education, Culture, and Identity in Twentieth-Century China. Glen Peterson, Ruth Hayhoe, and Yongling Lu, eds. p.187–192. Ann Arbor, MI: University of Michigan Press.

Thomas, Murray R., ed. 1998 Oriental Theories of Human Development. New York: Peter Lang.

Tian, Rong. 1997 Chengdushi Qingnian Sixiang Guannian De Xin Bianhua (Ideology and Thought Change among Youth in Chengdu). Qingnian Yanjou (Research on Youth) July 1997:29–31.

Tsai, Yu Jen. 1994 The Interactions between China's Politics and Education in the Post-Mao Era. Ph.D. dissertation. University of Southern California.

Tran, Van Doan. 1991 Ideological Education and Moral Education. *In* Chinese Foundation for Moral Education and Character Development. Tran Van Doan, Vincent Shen and George F. Mclean, eds. p.113–153. Washington D.C.: Council for Research in Values and Philosophy.

Triandis, Harry. 1989 Cross-cultural Studies of Individualism and Collectivism. *In* Nebraska Symposium on Motivation, Vol. 37. Richard A. Dienstbier and John J. Berman, eds. p. 41–133. Lincoln, NE: University of Nebraska Press.

Tu, Wei-Ming, ed. 1994 China in Transformation. Cambridge, MA: Harvard University Press.

Walker, Lawrence J. and Thomas J. Moran. 1991 Moral Reasoning in a Communist Chinese Society. Journal of Moral Education 20(2):139–155.

Wang, Jia. 1985 Deyu (Moral Education). *In* Zhongguo Da Baike Quan Shu Jiaoyu Juan (Great Encyclopedia of China: Education). Qiaomu Hu, ed. p.1985:59–60. Beijing, China: Zhongguo Da Baike Quan Shu Chubanshe.

Wang, Jingtang. 1988 Deyu De Kunjing Yu Chulu (The Dilemma and Way Out of Moral Education). Jiaoyu Yanjou (Educational Research) December 1988:51–53.

Wang, Huanli and Yixian Li. 1985 Daode Pinzhi Jiaoyu (Moral Trait Education). *In* Zhongguo Da Baike Quan Shu Jiaoyu Juan (Great Encyclopedia of China:

Education). Hu Qiaomu, ed. p. 47–48. Beijing, China: Zhongguo Da Baike Quan Shu Chubanshe.

Webb, Keane. 1997 Signs of Recognition: Powers and Hazards of Representation in an Indonesian Society. Los Angeles: University of California Press.

Wei, Xianchao. 1995 Zhengti Dadeyu Kecheng Tixi Cutan (A Study on the Overall System of the Inclusive Moral Education Curriculum). Jiaoyu Yanjiu (Educational Research) October 1995:48–54.

White, Gordon. 1995 The Decline of Ideocracy. *In* China in the 1990s. Robert Benewick and Paul Wingrove, eds. p. 21–33. Vancouver, Canada: UBS Press.

Whyte, Martin King. 1974 Small Groups and Political Rituals in China. Berkeley, CA: University of California Press.

Wilson, Richard W. 1970 Learning to Be Chinese: The Political Socialization of Children in Taiwan. Cambridge, MA: The MIT Press.

Wilson, Richard W., Sidney L. Greenblatt, and Amy Auerbacher Wilson, eds. 1981 Moral Behavior in Chinese Society. New York: Praeger.

Wong, Linda and Ka-ho Mok. 1995 The Reform and the Changing Social Context. *In* Social Change and Social Policy in Contemporary China. Linda Wong and Stewart MacPherson, eds. p. 1–26. Aldershot, England: Avebury.

Wu, Qiuli. 1992 The Application of Modeling as an Approach to Conduct Moral Education in the People's Republic of China. Ph.D. dissertation. Ohio University.

Yang, Guoshu and Anbang Zhu, eds. 1994 Zhongguoren De Xinli Yu Xingwei (The Psychology and Behavior of the Chinese People. 2nd ed. Taibei, Taiwan: Gui Guan Tu Shu Gong Si.

Yeh, Milton D. 1988 The Ideology and Politics of Teng's Leadership in Post-Mao Mainland China. *In* Ideology and Politics in Twentieth-Century China. King-Yuh Chang, ed. p. 116–130. Taipei, Taiwan: National Chengchi University.

Yuan, Zheng. The Status of Confucianism in Modern Chinese Education 1901–1949: A Curricular Study. *In* Education, Culture, and Identity in Twentieth-Century China. Glen Peterson, Ruth Hayhoe, and Yongling Lu, eds. pp. 193–216. Ann Arbor, MI: University of Michigan Press.

Zagorin, Perez. 1990 Ways of Lying. Cambridge, MA: Harvard University Press.

Zhang, Chunhou and C. Edwin Vaughan. 1996 Student Responses to Economic Reform in China. Adolescence 31 (123):663–677.

Zhang, Huzheng and Laigui Lu. 1996 Zhonggong Lixiang Renge De Shuzao (The Molding of Chinese Communist Ideal Personality). *In* Daode Yu Gongmin Jiaoyu (Morality and Citizenship Education). Guoqiang Liu and Ruiquan Li, eds. pp.165–198. Hong Kong: Hong Kong Institute of Educational Research.

Zhang, Tianbao. 2000 Shilun Zhutixing Jiaoyu De Jiben Liyan (A Study on the Basic Concept of Subject-oriented Education). Jiaoyu Yanjiu (Educational Research) August 2000:13–18.

Zhao, Li. 1998 Personal Work Report. (Files of the Author)

Zhu, Xiaoman. 1996 Zhongguo Chuantong De Qingganxing Daode Jiaoyu Jiqi Muoshi (The ChineseTransitional Model for Affection and Moral Education). Jiaoyu Yanjiu (Educational Research) September 1996:30–48.
———. 2000 Yude Shi Jiaoyu De Linghun Dongqing Shi Deyu De Guanjian (Arousing of Emotion as the Key Link of Moral Education). Jiaoyu Yanjiu (Educational Research) April 2000:7–8.

## ABOUT THE AUTHOR

Dr. Hongping Annie Nie is a language instructor at the Institute for Chinese Studies, University of Oxford, United Kingdom. She is also a tutor of Politics in Contemporary China at the University of Oxford. Born in China, Dr. Hongping Annie Nie was trained as an English teacher. She taught secondary school for seven years in China before pursuing graduate studies in the Untied States, where she received a Masters of Education in Curriculum & Instruction (Calvin College) and a Ph. D. in Cross-Cultural Education (Biola University).